ALSO BY A.K. TURNER

This Little Piggy Went to the Liquor Store

Mommy Had a Little Flask

Drinking with Dead Women Writers (with Elaine Ambrose)

Drinking with Dead Drunks (with Elaine Ambrose)

Hair of the Corn Dog

A.K. Turner

FEVER STREAK PRESS

FEVER STREAK PRESS

ISBN: 978-0-9913759-2-9

Design by Sarah Tregay, DesignWorks, Inc.
Author photo by LeAna Earley

For Elizabeth Day

CONTENTS

CHAPTER ONE

Humpin' Hannah's

Humpin' Hannah's seems determined to communicate via its name that it welcomes all manner of people, especially those without class and with questionable hygiene. If you're in from out of town and want a slightly rednecky place to have a few beers and maybe win a dildo, then it's perfect. These days, I'd like to hold my head high and say with confidence that I don't hang out at a place that awards plastic replicas of the male genitalia to the most enthusiastic dancers. And I'm all for dildos, really. I'm no prude.

If a bar has Humpin' in the name, I'm compelled to object. First of all, is it so hard to pronounce the *g*? And what is the object of the phrase, as in humpin' Hannah's *what*? What is it of Hannah's that's being humped? Or is Hannah the humper? Does she hump compulsively? Is there a support group that might be of some help to her? Is she a promiscuous young lady? Or a dog that behaves inappropriately with the legs of guests at her master's dinner parties?

Humpin' Hannah sounds like she might be a good fit for Dirty Little Roddy, whose establishment is just a block or so away. While a few drinks topped off with a dollop of peer pressure can convince me to enter Humpin' Hannah's, I've made a solemn vow to never again frequent Dirty Little Roddy's. I'm way too uptight and pretentious to hang out at a place that doesn't even try to be clean—and instead proudly proclaims its filth in its name. Of course, I wasn't always so uptight and pretentious, and in our first few years in Boise, I went there a handful of times with friends. This was before children. My level of accepted debauchery lowered once I became a parent. Not that a baby would ever know I'd been to Dirty Little Roddy's, but still. It seems wrong to give birth and be responsible for the welfare of a new life in this world, only to get a babysitter so that I can get drunk on vodka and Red Bull while riding a mechanical bull at a smelly bar. If I'm going to hire a babysitter to go out, I want overpriced drinks and marble floors, damn it.

Maybe Humpin' Hannah is too good for Dirty Little Roddy, I thought as we entered. The place didn't look so bad. I was accompanied by my husband, Mike, and Kelly, an old friend, all-around good guy, and occasional drinking buddy. We played a few games of pool and drank horrible mixed drinks (how do you screw up a rum and coke?) until realizing that beer was the safer option. The band readied itself for the evening. I'd heard that the lead singer was also the owner of the club. By owning the establishment, she guaranteed that her band would headline the show every Friday and Saturday night. I'm sure in her day, she was quite the rocker. She had the figure and the moves of a younger version of herself, yet her voice strained to keep up, and I wondered how many more years of it she had in her. Incidentally, her name was not Hannah.

A group of bikers from Utah invaded the place, and I felt a slight apprehension for Kelly. He's a big guy and often the target of little guys with something to prove. Not that bikers from Utah are little guys with something to prove. But whenever anyone portrays outward aggression, I fear for Kelly. People pick fights with him.

Kelly loves to dance. He's good at many things, and dancing ranks pretty high on the list. But he's single and doesn't often have someone with whom to dance. So Kelly and I took to the dance floor, probably for something along the lines of "Brown-Eyed Girl" or "Sweet Home Alabama," one of those songs that people my age have heard about five thousand times too many. Kelly was a good dancer, and I was able to follow, if clumsily so. But Kelly may have had a few too many drinks at that point. He spun me around, our hands missed each other on the catch, and I watched in horror as Kelly lumbered backwards in slow motion. I felt like I should scream "Timber!" to the dance floor, but there was no way I'd be heard above the band. A bouncer standing off to the side eyed us narrowly as Kelly came crashing down, bumping into a group of the bikers and their girlfriends along the way. I immediately began a chorus of "Sorry, so sorry," and hoped that no one would start swinging. Kelly got to his feet, and we moved farther from the crowd to finish out the song. No one approached with brass knuckles and a puffed-up chest to avenge their tarnished honor, and I breathed a sigh of relief, though one of the girls did sneer at us, as if we'd set out to bump her and therefore ruin her night. I wanted to tell her that when she sneered like that, she was terribly unattractive, but then I remembered that I'm an adult, so I bit my tongue.

Mike and I danced to a few songs and then, giving each other *the look*, agreed that we were done. We bade farewell to Kelly, who wanted to stay out later, and left to find a cab.

On the drive home, I said to Mike, "I hope he's going to be all right."

"Don't worry," Mike said. "I'm sure he'll be fine."

"Who are you worried about?" the cabbie asked.

"We left a friend back there at a bar," Mike explained.

"And he's kind of drunk," I added.

"And he's a really big guy, and sometimes people pick fights with him," Mike said.

"And he's single and by himself." As I spoke, a frown took hold of my face.

"And we left him in a bar full of bikers," Mike concluded.

Mike and I looked at each other, and the more we voiced the facts of the situation, the more we felt like horrible parents, as if Kelly was our baby and we'd abandoned him in the company of dangerous strangers.

"I'm sure your buddy will be fine," said the cabbie. An identification card listed his name as Ryan.

"I bet you see some pretty crazy stuff," I said, partly because I was interested, partly because I wanted to switch the subject from Kelly's welfare, but mostly because this is what I do when we take cabs home. I ask the drivers to tell me stories about crazy, drunk people, because it makes me feel that however horribly I've screwed up in my life, I've never been *that* bad. Hearing stories of the bad behavior of others makes me feel less alone in the world. And a little bit better about myself.

"I once had a couple pay me to drive around while they screwed in the backseat."

"No way!" I said.

"I swear. They used to call me all the time to take them different places. Then one night they called and asked if I could pick them up from their house because they were going out to celebrate their fifteenth wedding anniversary. So I pick them up, and as I'm driving them to a restaurant, they say to me, 'We plan on getting a little crazy, so if we shock you, don't freak out.'"

"What did you think that meant?" I asked.

"I really had no idea. So I take them to this restaurant, and they call me again a few other times throughout the night. Restaurant to bar. Bar to bikini bar. Bikini bar to home."

"What's a bikini bar?" I asked.

"You know, like a strip club," Mike said.

"Oh right." I nodded. "You mean like the Idaho equivalent of a strip club." In Idaho, you can either serve alcohol or have naked dancers, but not both. This doesn't work that well for the places with naked dancers because it turns out that most people want to be drunk for sexploitation.

"So, I pick them up from the bikini bar and take them home, and I'm driving along, and all the sudden it gets really quiet. Like something's changed. Then my seat lurches forward. He's basically lifted her up and put her on his lap."

"What did you do?" Mike asked.

"I just kept driving." Ryan shrugged. "A minute later, she lies down in between the seats, so if I look down to my right as I'm driving, there's her head looking up at me. And her dress is hiked up, and she's all exposed, and he goes down on her. This lasts maybe four or five minutes. She's holding on to each of the seats to keep herself steady. At one point, I look at her, and her dress is covering half her face, and I can see one eye peering up at me, and she says, 'A little help here,' so I reach over and pull her dress back down a little bit so it's not covering her face and exposing the rest of her. The guy sits up in the backseat and gives me a thumbs up in the rear-view mirror. Then the guy pulls her into the backseat, and they actually start having sex. He has his back to me; she's sitting on the seat and has her legs up over his shoulders. And one of her feet actually rests right here." He motioned to the space right next to his head. "And they're really going for it. I mean, the sounds, the smells, it's all there."

"Ew," I said.

"So then we're almost to their house, so I said, 'We're almost home, kids. What do you want to do?' And the windows are actually fogging up, so I crack a window. The woman says, 'My mom's in there with the kids. Just keep circling.' So I do, and then I can tell…" As Ryan drives, he holds his hand up in the air, the motion people make when they don't actually have words and hope a gesture will suffice.

"They finished?" Mike said. At that moment, it occurred to me that we were hearing a story of strangers coupling in the very place where we were seated.

"They finished," Ryan confirmed. "So I pull up to their house, and the guy says, 'Let me get her inside and come right back out and pay you.'"

"Don't you dare tell me they stiffed you!" I demanded.

"Nope, the guy came back with baby wipes, cleaned the car, and gave me a $125 tip."

"Did you ever hear from them again?" I asked.

"Nope. Never called me once after that."

"You get a lot of regular customers?" Mike asked.

"Some. There was a prostitute who used to call a lot."

"How do you know she was a prostitute?" I asked, and then instantly regretted it. Maybe I didn't want to know how he knew.

"She used to have me pick her up at her house, and she'd always say she was going to her boyfriend's house. But it was always a different house, and she never knew how to get there, so we always had to use the GPS."

"Yeah, that's probably a good indication," I agreed.

"One day I pick her up from her house, which was, let's just say, not in a nice neighborhood. When I pull up to her house, she has a garden hose in her hand, and she's spraying water on a group of people running away. She puts down the hose, gets in the car, and I said, 'What was that? Why were you spraying those people?' And I'm kind of wondering if the cops are going to show after this little altercation I've witnessed, and I don't want to be accused of being a getaway car, so I decide I'm not taking her anywhere until I hear some sort of explanation for what I just saw. She tells me that she's been hearing voices, and she's been off meth for six months."

"Oh god," I said, suddenly feeling like a really stellar passenger.

"She says it had been getting worse, and she thought someone was in the crawlspace of her house, but she was always too afraid to check by herself. So one day she calls the cops, they come out to her house, hear her story, and blow her off. Honestly, it's easy to see how that would happen. But then she says the voices get worse still, and now they're taunting her because they know the cops won't do anything. They're knocking on the floor and stuff like that. She even sees a glow coming up from the floorboards, like there are lights down there. So she took her garden hose and started pouring water down through the vents and then took it outside and turned it on full blast into the crawlspace. A family of five came running out, and that's who she was spraying when I pulled up."

"They were living there?" I asked.

"Well, that's what she said, but honestly, with the looks of her and the place where she lives and the druggie past and all, I'm not inclined to believe much that she says. So I call bullshit. And we're still parked outside of her house. So she says, 'I'll show you.'"

"And you looked?" Mike asked.

"I totally looked," said Ryan. "It was like a twenty by twenty space under her house, only about three feet high. There was a blow-up mattress down there. There was a coffee table and end tables, and they were normal size except the legs had been sawed off so that they only stood about six inches off the ground. They'd tapped into her power, they had a microwave. They'd tapped into her cable, they had a television."

"That is the creepiest fucking thing I've ever heard," I said.

"So we get back in the cab, and I asked her, 'What are you going to do now? You just pissed off the people who were living under your house.' I mean, I would be scared. And she looks at me, and she just says, 'I'm gonna go stay with my boyfriend for a week.'"

"Jesus, you have some stories," said Mike.

"I had a ninja puker once."

"I'm not sure what that means," I confessed.

"Well, it was a girl who was really drunk, and she promised not to puke in my car. And I didn't think she'd puked."

"But she did?"

"This girl was so stealthy, I never even realized she puked until I went through a drive-thru later and someone asked me what happened to the side of my car. The whole side of it was plastered. But hey, she didn't puke on the interior, so it's all good." I realized that my definition of "all good" would have to change significantly if I ever drove a cab.

The next day, I waited until late afternoon to call Kelly and see how he'd fared the night before. I wanted to make sure he was still alive, that he hadn't been beaten up by bikers and left in an alley. I'm not assuming that the bikers were bad people. They could have been Mormon bikers for all I know. Actually, strike that. I'm sure there are Mormon bikers out there, but I don't think they pound beer and dance for dildos. And I don't like to think of myself as someone who judges others on appearance alone, but if you're trying to look tough and aggressive, I'm at least going to assume you are aggressive, and that appeared to be the case in the situation at Humpin' Hannah's. When I finally got a hold of Kelly, he was, indeed, alive.

"Oh..." he mumbled.

"Kelly?"

"Yeah..." He did not sound good.

"I just wanted to make sure you made it home last night."

"Yeah, yeah I did. I stayed for a little longer. And then I

was headed home, but when I got home, my neighbors were throwing a party."

"Oh no." Kelly's neighbors are four college kids and technically his tenants. I'm not saying that we didn't party like they do when we were back in college, but that was fifteen years ago. And one's ability to keep up dwindles over time.

"I remember drinking shots of tequila," Kelly continued.

"That's not good."

"No, no it's not. But they had some girls over. And they were all playing beer pong. And I remember they were playing strip beer pong."

I confess that I do not know what beer pong is, have never played beer pong, and I have no intention of ever doing so. Though I'm sure I'd be fantastic at it. I can only assume that beer pong is an updated version of what we called quarters back in my day. I'm not sure what strip beer pong entails, but I assume that in addition to getting drunk, you get naked.

"And the girls were losing," Kelly continued. "So that was cool."

"So you watched a bunch of college kids get drunk and naked."

"Let's call them men and women."

"Don't want to be the creepy landlord?"

"No, no I don't."

"Okay, so you watched a bunch of men get naked," I said. "*Amanda!*"

"Sorry, couldn't resist."

"And then they were talking about shotgunning beer. And I told them they didn't stand a chance against me."

"And did they stand a chance?"

"Are you forgetting that I played rugby?" Kelly asked.

Kelly and Mike played rugby together in college. The goal of joining a rugby team is to make it through the season with really cool scars, but without an actual visit to the hospital, and to get rip-roaring drunk with great frequency.

But rugby players don't just drink shots or shotgun beer. They put various substances, like alcohol and spit, into the cleat of the biggest player on the team. And those who score a try (like a goal, only the rugby version) have to drink this disgusting and likely dangerous concoction at the party afterward. It's a stupid ritual, accompanied by chants from the teammates of "Shoot the boot! Shoot the boot!" If I had been in that scenario, I would purposefully have been a horrific rugby player.

Lucky for Mike, he had me. He would often skip the after-party, telling his teammates that he couldn't go because he had to go home with "the wife." This was a total lie. I was more of a partier than my husband and would gladly have gotten drunk with the rugby team, especially since no one was going to ask me to shoot the boot. But I encouraged my husband to lie and blame me for the fact that he couldn't party after the game, because I could tell that the idea of shooting the boot and some of the other rugby rituals were as disgusting to him as they were to me.

Kelly, on the other hand, was not married, and when he and Mike played rugby together, Kelly often attended the after-party and took his already impressive drinking skills to new heights.

"So you put the college kids to shame then?" I asked.

"Yeah." He groaned. "But do me a favor."

"Sure thing."

"Next time we go out, and you guys are ready to go home, make me go home, too."

I gave Kelly my word, just as I'd vowed the night before to carry some sort of plastic sheeting with me at all times from that point forward. It had to be small enough to fit in my purse, but large enough to cover the backseat of a standard cab.

* * *

CHAPTER TWO

The Breakup

"You know who would love Humpin' Hannah's?" I asked.

"My parents," said Mike.

It's not that my in-laws don't have standards; it's that they have different standards. And they never shy away from a place that uses crude innuendo as a selling point. They're likely to think the name Humpin' Hannah's is cute. Their main requirement for a fun place to go out is that it has a good beat and room to dance. In that regard, Humpin' Hannah's would be perfect for them. They are fantastic dancers, and if they accidentally bumped into someone, that person wouldn't dare sneer at them. Unlike the towering figure of Kelly, both my mother-in-law and father-in-law are short. As a couple, they are terribly cute, and when they dance, even more so. And somehow I don't think they'd bat an eye at the band handing out dildos. On the contrary, they'd just congratulate the winners. I can picture my mother-in-law relating the events as follows: "The band gave dildos to the audience, isn't that nice?" She'd say this with the same inflection that you'd imagine other women her age using when discussing knitting or baking.

My in-laws typically spend a large portion of the summers with us in Boise. We have a downstairs bedroom and bathroom that are hardly used otherwise, and they can escape the heat of Mexico, where they live the rest of the year. All three of their children have settled in Boise, so it allows them to have family time with kids and grandkids.

I don't expect my brother-in-law Virgil to ever be able to accommodate his parents for a portion of the summers, but my sister-in-law, Sandi, and her husband, Matt, have plenty of room at their house.

"So, Sandi," I casually mentioned over the phone, "when is your guestroom going to be finished?" Sandi and Matt's home has an unfinished basement that will someday be a guestroom and hopefully an alternative location at which my in-laws can set up camp for the summer.

"By next year, for sure," she assured me, just as she assures me every year. "Matt just needs to finish it."

Matt and Sandi are known for living in a state of chaos. I think they share the blame equally. While Matt might take longer than would be expected to finish a project, sometimes that's because there is simply too much stuff in the way. Both Matt and Sandi are collectors who border on hoarding, though both would say so only about their spouse. Sandi possesses more clothes than anyone else I know. She has more clothes than she can possibly ever wear, yet continues to shop.

"Look at this scarf," she'll say, showing me something that is likely very hip but nothing I would ever wear. "I got it on sale."

The words "on sale" compel her to purchase. Even if she already owns 280 other scarves. And really, you can only wear one scarf at a time, right? I'm not even talking about a scarf with any practical attributes. This isn't something that you can wrap around your head and neck for warmth; this is strictly an accessory, a wispy strip of gauze. If her compulsion to purchase things was limited to scarves, that would be okay, but she's the same with shoes, jackets, skirts, blouses, dresses, and any other item of clothing a woman could wear. She requires the equivalent of a studio apartment to maintain her wardrobe.

Matt, on the other hand, hoards more manly things. I wasn't aware of this until one day when I asked Sandi why they never parked in their garage.

"We can't," she explained. "That's where Matt keeps all of his parts for exercise bikes."

"You guys have an exercise bike?"

"No."

"Are you going to get one?"

"No."

"Is he starting an exercise bike repair business?"

"No."

"Then why does he have a garage full of parts?"

"I don't know. Want to see what I just got on sale?"

Matt is a compulsive thrift store shopper as well, buying all sorts of useless crap that might one day never come in handy. Both Matt and Sandi's hoarding could still be manageable if it didn't apply to their kids' stuff, too. If Sandi had a ridiculous closet, and Matt junked up his garage, that would be one thing. But Sandi's addiction to purchasing clothing combined with Matt's addiction to thrift stores has created the perfect storm. Sandi shops for her girls. Matt also shops for his daughters, at thrift stores. The end result is that my nieces have more clothing than should be allowed by law. When one seven-year-old girl owns thirty-two leotards, you know things have gotten out of hand. After all, you can only wear one leotard at a time, right? Or at least, you *should* wear only one leotard at a time.

I don't bitch about this, because it has created a steady stream of free clothing for my girls. Emilia and Ivy are younger by a few years than their cousins. So when Matt and Sandi must thin their daughters' closets to make way for a new load of clothing, my daughters inherit trash bags full of clothing, which means I never have to spend a dime on clothing my children. Well, okay, sometimes I have to buy shoes because my daughters' feet are oddly shaped, and unless we're surviving under the poverty line, I won't make my kids wear hand-me-down underwear. Actually, even if we're homeless, I will still find a way to buy my daughters new underwear, because I just find recycling it entirely wrong.

Because of various factors including hoarding, procrastination, time, and money, Matt and Sandi have never, and may never, finish their basement. There is no room at their house for my in-laws to stay, which means that Mike and I end up with his parents as extended houseguests every summer.

One of the great things about having my father-in-law around is that he will spend hours landscaping our property. Although, one of the bad things about having my father-in-law around is that he will spend hours landscaping our property. When someone is performing free manual labor for you, it's difficult to complain, so instead, I've just asked that he limit how much landscaping he does. Part of the problem is that he gets extremely cut-happy. He'll begin trimming a tree, but then become so engrossed in what he's doing that before you know it, he's cut something so far back that it looks like a pathetic, twig rendition of its former self. He over cuts, partly because he's used to landscaping his plants in Mexico, where things grow more rapidly than in Idaho. And when he hacks away at an undeserving tree, he then piles the trimmings into a massive mess of branches that are left to rot along the side of our property.

"You want me to trim your ivy again?" he asked.

My eyes grew wide with fear, and I turned to Mike.

"Dad," Mike interjected, "we're not trimming the ivy anymore. Ever again."

The last time my father-in-law had trimmed the ivy on the front of our house, he'd formed it into one thick line, razor-straight, running from the ground to the roof. Unfortunately, when he was finished, we had what looked like a landing strip on the front of our house, and whenever I arrived home, all I could think of was a giant, green pubic hair strip attacking our home. I thought that everyone saw this, that others were as appalled as me, but I was alone in this. What kind of person looks at a line of trimmed ivy and thinks of the standard American adult film star landing strip? Apparently, my kind of person.

When the pubic strip grew out a bit and stopped looking quite so pornographic and again took on the organic lines of a living plant, we decided the ivy needed to come out entirely. It was causing too much destruction to our home, as ivy is prone to do. Given the difficulty and lack of sleep that Ivy, our second born, caused us during her first three years of life, I decided she was appropriately named.

"I'll do it!" my father-in-law volunteered when we told him the ivy could go.

He completed this job so efficiently and with such attention to detail, both throwing away all of the clippings and cleaning up the damage to the house, including scraping and painting, we decided that this was more the type of job he should be tasked with in the future. Trimming something is not his forte, but when it comes to destroying something entirely, he's gifted. I wondered if we had anything else that needed to be obliterated, something to keep him occupied on his impending visit.

"Amanda," my father-in-law said on the first night of his arrival. He'd come alone, as my mother-in-law was visiting family in Washington and would show up a few days later. "Do you think tomorrow morning you could run me up to the storage unit?"

"Of course," I said. My schedule was fairly open on my father-in-law's first full day in town. They'd rented a storage unit in Boise so as not to completely overrun our house and garage with their belongings. It came in especially handy when, a few years prior, they'd purchased a small, used sports car so that they'd have a fun vehicle to tool around with in the summers, something other than the mammoth truck they use to commute from Mexico to Idaho and back again. For the first two years they had it, my father-in-law was smitten with this car. It was a convertible, an older model Honda that he spent hours polishing and buffing in our driveway. He would shine it up, make himself a martini, and drag others out to the car so that we could take pictures of him in the driver's seat with a martini in hand. This was in no way meant to advocate drinking and driving, and the ridiculousness of sitting in the driver's seat while holding a martini never really occurred to him. He simply wanted a picture to show off to friends and relatives, one that expressed that life was good. And the best way that he could think of to communicate this was through a sports car and a martini. If he could combine the two into one picture, then so be it.

"Does anyone else see how utterly wrong this picture is?" I whispered to Mike when my father-in-law was showing it off.

"Yes," Mike muttered back. "But *he* doesn't, so just let him enjoy it."

The morning after my father-in-law's arrival, I drove him to the storage unit. After five minutes of fiddling with the lock and various keys, we got it open. He smiled at the car, but I noticed something different about the way he looked at it. His previous exuberance had diminished.

He hooked up the battery, started the car, and drove it out of the storage unit. When he got out of the car, he and I looked at the concrete where the car had been parked. It was wet. Something had leaked.

"Hmm," he said with dismay, staring at the stain. At that moment, I knew he'd fallen out of love with the car. It was as if she'd pissed on him. If he'd had a rolled-up newspaper in hand, I felt certain he'd have whacked the little sports car on the hood.

He drove the car back to our house, where it sat for most of the summer. He hardly doted on it as he used to and almost always opted to drive his mammoth truck instead of the little convertible.

My mother-in-law arrived a few days later.

"Well, I guess he's done with the sports car," she remarked.

"I guess so. It makes me kind of sad," I admitted. "I feel like I should make him a martini and offer to take his picture behind the wheel."

"What are you two talking about?" Mike asked as he entered the kitchen.

"How your dad fell out of love with the car," I said.

"Yeah." Mike shook his head in sadness. "It's surprising. I didn't see that coming." He spoke solemnly, as if discussing close friends having announced their impending divorce.

"Maybe you two need a little sports car to tool around in?" my mother-in-law suggested.

"Fuck no," Mike blurted.

"Sorry, Nana," I confirmed. "Mike and I have always hated driving that car."

"Me, too," she admitted in a whisper. "But don't tell my husband."

"What are we having?" my father-in-law said as he joined us in the kitchen and nodded to a large saucepan simmering on the stove.

"Coconut curry chicken," I answered with pride.

"Ooh. That sounds delicious." As he said this, he opened the refrigerator and took out a sampling of various "kid" foods. By "kid" foods, I mean the food that we use to pack the kids' lunches, not necessarily food we eat ourselves, like vanilla yogurt and string cheese. He ate straight from a gigantic tub of vanilla yogurt, and I made a mental note that it was now Papa's vanilla yogurt.

As my coconut curry chicken simmered, my father-in-law stood in the kitchen and wrestled with string cheese. Mike and I stared at him as he tried, and failed, to extract the cheese from the wrapper.

"Dad, do you want some help?" Mike asked.

"No," my father-in-law answered.

"Because I'm sure Ivy could open that for you. She's four, you know."

My father-in-law glared at his son while I handed him a pair of scissors.

"The wrapper somehow got com-promised."

What promised? I wondered. I looked to Mike, and we smirked at each other, realizing that my father-in-law had somehow come up with a new pronunciation of *compromised*. I'd never heard that particular version before.

"So, what do you guys have planned over the next month?" Mike asked.

"Well, we have a lot of socializing to do," Papa said.

"What can I say," Nana added. "We like to party."

"We don't party that hard," Papa fired back. "Not compared to some of our friends."

"Are you kidding?" I interjected. "You guys party a lot."

"But we're relatively tame," my father-in-law said. "I mean, we've never done cocaine." He looked thoughtful for a moment and then stared at his wife and added, "I'm assuming you've never done cocaine?"

"It's a good thing you were such a good kid growing up," Nana said to Mike, ignoring her husband's inquiry. "We never really had to worry about you."

"Ha!" said Mike. "You just believed whatever I told you. And you were too busy teaching, coaching, and partying to pay attention to all that was going on."

"That's not true," Papa chided. "I just think that compared to your siblings, we got the impression we didn't have to worry about you as much."

"Well that's true," Mike confirmed. "Compared to my siblings, you didn't."

Sandi spent much of her youth sneaking out of the house and partying like a rock star, while Virgil was the handful that every parent fears and that no one knows how to deal with.

"You know, Mike passed more than one field sobriety test in the driveway of your house," I said.

"What?" Nana seemed shocked.

"Yeah," Mike confirmed. "The police were always trying to bust me for something. They'd follow me home, and more than once they gave me the drunk test in our driveway."

"Where were we?" Nana asked.

Mike shrugged.

"But they never nailed you?" she asked.

"No, because I knew if I ever screwed up, I'd never get off that rock." The rock he spoke of was the town of Sitka, Alaska. Mike grew up with the fear that if he didn't get a scholarship, go to college, and find a way to venture further out into the world, he'd spend the rest of his life mowing lawns in the rain, which is how he spent much of his youth. "But I was only good from tenth grade on, because that was when I started to get scared about the prospect of being stuck there all my life. Before that, I got into all kinds of trouble. But I'd watch my friends work their asses off at these jobs and then spend every cent on booze and pot. It just seemed so dumb."

"Wait," Papa interjected. "I'm still digesting the part about you getting a field sobriety test in our driveway."

"Grandma Turner came out of the house in the middle of one," Mike suddenly remembered.

Papa looked perplexed as he imagined his mother watching her grandson touch his nose with his eyes closed in the driveway of his home. He seemed to make peace with this image and then announced, "I'm going to have a martini. Does anyone else want one?"

My in-laws are the busiest retired people I know. When I picture retirement, sure I picture a lot of travel, but I also picture some sedentary activities, which I know causes panic in my husband. I have every intention of staying active, and there's no way I will turn into a blob in a recliner watching *Wheel of Fortune* until death mercifully comes, but I also look forward to doing a crossword puzzle or a jigsaw puzzle. Okay, I secretly want to become a puzzle addict, but there doesn't seem to be time for that with the hectic life that is my current reality. I don't think you'll ever catch my in-laws spending hours brooding over a five-thousand-piece puzzle of the Eiffel Tower. It's just not their thing. Not that they can't sit down and relax. They churn through novels like nobody's business, and they love to sit and watch movies together. By sit and watch, I actually mean sit and nap in front of a movie and later talk about how much they enjoyed it.

They are in the latter half of their sixties but fill their time with mountain biking, kayak trips, hunting, cruises, and teaching Zumba. Okay, this last one belongs exclusively to my mother-in-law. They outlined their plans, and I knew that between their own itineraries and the things I wanted to do before the school year started, we had a busy summer ahead.

When they left for a three-day trip to California, Mike and I took the opportunity to do a three-day health binge. It was something we'd wanted to do, but we wouldn't dare do it in the presence of my in-laws. We find it difficult not to drink around Nana and Papa. Not that they drive us to the bottle, but because we naturally associate them with cocktails and good times.

We called it a "modified fast" because that sounded more sophisticated and effective than "three-day diet." For three days, we would survive on nothing but health shakes, the ingredients of which are spinach, almond milk, carrot juice, banana, frozen fruit, and chocolate protein powder. This may sound like a disgusting combination, but you can put just about anything in a blender, and as long as you top it off with chocolate protein powder, it will come out tasting like a chocolate milkshake. It will not, however, come out looking like a chocolate milkshake, as the combination of spinach, carrot juice, and protein powder yields an unholy hue. It is a drink well-suited to the colorblind community.

Our motivation for the three-day health binge was general detoxification or at least non-toxification. Even if we didn't decrease the level of toxins in our bodies, at least we wouldn't increase them. Three days sounded like an eternity of starvation to me, yet I sensed Mike's disappointment with me for not committing to seven.

"You do whatever you want," I said, "but I think three days is plenty."

"It's not going to be as hard as you think," he insisted.

"You'll be amazed at how your body adapts. You might feel hungry at first, but then that goes away. Believe me, I've screwed with my body enough to know how this works." He spoke of his experience in high school on the wrestling team, that strange storm of boys, anorexia, and sport.

"That was twenty years ago," I pointed out. "Your body might be different now. In any case, I'm only committing to three days."

"Fine," he agreed. "But at the end of the three days, I bet we'll decide to keep it going a bit longer."

The prospect of surviving off of health shakes and water brought out Mike's glass-is-half-full optimism and my glass-is-bone-dry pessimism.

"I'm *so* hungry," Mike whined at the end of Day One.

"Really? I'm not having a problem," I said smugly. "Do you want another shake?"

"I'm sick of the shakes. I hate the shakes."

"What? You *love* the shakes. You wanted to live off the shakes for a *week,* remember?"

My attitude evaporated by Day Two. He came home in the afternoon to find me listless on the couch. "Are you okay?" he asked.

"I'm *so* tired," I groaned. I was sprawled out, staring at my computer as if that equated to actual work.

"Maybe you'll feel better if you get up and move around," he suggested. This is Mike's go-to solution for ailments. If I am ill or tired or in any condition for which the only remedy is rest, he prescribes movement. I find this illogic maddening and engineered to induce guilt regarding my lethargy. If I'd had the energy, I would have told him so.

In the late afternoon of Day Three, Mike said, "So, you know, we've pretty much *done* this."

"What do you mean?"

"I mean, I think we can call it good. That's close enough. Maybe we should take the girls out for pizza?"

"And beer?"

"Well, we don't have to get beer," he said.

"If we go to the pizza place and eat pizza, I'm getting a beer to go with it."

"Okay."

"That's non-negotiable."

"Okay."

"Otherwise, I say let's just keep going and complete the full three days. *I* can make it. I want to make that clear."

"Let's go out for pizza and beer," he said.

"Okay."

Halfway through the glorious meal, Mike disappeared for a disturbingly long time to the bathroom.

"Do you feel okay?" he asked me on the way home.

"Are you kidding? I feel great! Pizza and beer was exactly what I needed. I feel whole again." My energy had returned, and the world seemed a wonderful place. "How about you?" I asked.

"Yeah, I threw up."

"Oh, honey, I'm sorry you're not feeling good."

And I was sorry. But I was also relieved that the three days, which we failed to complete, ended poorly for him, because he was less likely to want to do it again. And I learned from the experience that my body runs primarily on toxins.

* * *

CHAPTER THREE

On Towing a Body Down the River

One of the best activities to enjoy in the Boise summer is floating the river. The first time I'd heard this, I pictured people bobbing in inner tubes down a lazy, calm stretch of water. That or a discarded corpse. In the first vision, the inner tube part is correct, for those who don't mind permanently freezing the living cells in their buttocks. I suppose if you got cold enough, you could start the river as a tuber and end it as a corpse. Some of us prefer the security of a raft and paddles. In any case, the river is often anything but lazy. Small falls don't look menacing until you are about to go over them.

It took about five years of living in Boise before I floated the river, because I generally run on a five-year delay. This is true when it comes to technology, too. I was about five years late for email and Facebook, so I only have a few years to go before I finally get on Vine and Instagram and Snapchat.

My first float was an office trip with my husband and the other agents at his brokerage. We planned the trip as a way to celebrate Sandi's birthday, as she works at the office, too. I spent the trip furiously clutching two things. The first was my lifejacket. The clutching part wasn't really necessary, since the lifejacket was buckled firmly in place. To my dismay, most of my companions eschewed the lifejacket, whereas I will always choose looking ridiculous and living, as opposed to looking cool and drowning. Because think about it, if you drown and they don't find your body for a while, then when they do, you'll be bloated and possibly snacked on by river creatures, and then you'll really look uncool. But I get why people don't want to wear the life-saving device; the river is not very deep, a lifejacket is uncomfortable, et cetera. Still, I wore my lifejacket. I'd been a parent for a few years and therefore had many ominous phrases permanently etched into my brain about the dangers of children and water and how it takes only an inch of water for a person to drown. My skills in the water are equivalent to that of a small child, so I figured I'd better wear it. And I chalked my boat mates' behavior up to foolishness, for they too could drown in an inch of water. If you were thrown from the boat and knocked unconscious, your superior strength and swimming skills would do you about as much good in the river as a brick.

The second item to which I clung was the camera. This wasn't because I wanted to make sure I properly documented the trip, but because I didn't want anyone to have a chance to take a picture of me. Lifejackets are not very slimming, especially when they scrunch up your fat in certain parts, as if highlighting it specifically for the camera.

Since this was my first trip, it was my first exposure to some of the more dangerous parts of the river. There are sections where the current moves terribly fast and can suck you closer to the banks where menacing branches jut out ready to impale you. Our raft became victim to one such current and swept us into the bank. Sandi sat facing me, away from the direction we were heading. "Get down!" I yelled as the raft shot toward the branches. She and I hunched over, and a coworker was catapulted from the raft. As soon as I saw that we were minus one person, I began framing how I would relate his death to his wife, trying not to sound too smug about the fact that he should have been wearing a life-jacket like some people, but since he hadn't, there was nothing we could do when he was thrown from the boat, knocked unconscious, and drowned along the banks in a mere inch of water. Such a waste. But that didn't actually happen. In a much less exciting conclusion, he survived unharmed and climbed back in the raft.

We surveyed the damage. Everyone and the raft seemed to be intact, though Sandi huddled directly underneath a protruding and jagged branch that was two inches in diameter, waiting to spear an unsuspecting rafter. I don't ever want my sister-in-law to be impaled, but I especially don't want her to be impaled on her birthday.

In the two years after that first trip, Mike and I floated the river a handful of times. We became more comfortable with it and decided that our children were now old enough to join us. This may sound reckless in the wake of Sandi's near impalement, but we felt we had a good handle on the river, and our kids were big enough by that point to follow directions and stay safe. Nonetheless, I spent the entire trip holding both kids, who were firmly secured in lifejackets, in a vice-like grip to allay my fear of them falling out of the boat.

"Is that comfortable, Amanda?" Mike asked, knowing that it wasn't.

"I'm fine," I said.

"But are you having fun? This is supposed to be fun."

"I am having fun."

"You look uncomfortable and miserable."

"This is my fun face."

Ivy looked up at me and said, "You look mean, Mama."

"You don't have to hold the kids so tight. They're fine."

"Yeah, Mom." Emilia squirmed. "You're hurting me. Can't I just touch the water?"

"No!"

"I think our definitions of fun and enjoyment are different," Mike said.

"I just want to keep my kids safe," I insisted. It occurred to me then that while my kids might be ready to float the river, I was not ready for them to float the river.

We got out at one point along a sandy bank to stretch our legs. As we got back in the boat, I mistakenly bumped and opened one of the valves of the inflatable raft. The sickening sound of air leaving the raft rushed at me, and I panicked and furiously tried to close the valve. When I did so, I looked at Mike.

"Yeah," he said. "Try not to do that."

We continued on and rounded a bend where a group of pot smokers sat getting stoned and building rock sculptures. They'd done a great job at both, and Emilia and Ivy pointed to the sculptures excitedly.

"Ooh, can we stop there?" Emilia asked.

I looked at one of the stoners sitting in lotus position and inhaled the reek of marijuana drifting out over the water.

"I don't think so," I said.

We finished the trip with everyone safe and sound, and my confidence in terms of floating the river grew. Emilia and Ivy obeyed every command and kept their personal flotation devices on them at all times.

About a week later, Kelly stopped by. We stood chatting in the kitchen when he suddenly looked as if he'd remembered something very important.

"Hey," he said excitedly, "have you guys ever seen—" He fiddled with his phone, and I tried not to groan. I was sure he was going to show us a new app or drafting software or a picture of a gadget or a movie trailer for something sci-fi. "A liger," he continued, and then he held his phone up to display a picture of a liger.

I'd heard of a liger, that it was the resulting offspring from a lion and tiger getting it on. But I'd never before seen a picture. I'd never really wanted to. But now Kelly held up a picture of the most mammoth cat I'd ever seen in my life. And it was being cuddled by humans, ostensibly the humans who facilitated its existence and raised it. All I could think was that these humans had grown a bit cocky. Hadn't they heard what happened to Siegfried and Roy? Did they not follow the news stories of maulings that occur at zoos when drunk people taunt the animals and the animals react by proving that they can, in fact, get out whenever they want to? I could see why the ligers appealed to Kelly, because their creation and the potential damage they could do (to their creators, among others) was right in line with a good sci-fi plot.

There were pictures of the ligers playing, swimming, and standing up tall. Pictures of ligers lounging next to women with their cleavage on display. Pictures where people had their heads next to the ligers, to show the difference in size. The ligers looked roughly big enough to eat a full-grown man in three bites. Personally, I don't see the need to create any bigger cats than those which already exist in nature. Whenever I go to the zoo, I'm startled not only by the height of the tigers and the enormous heads of the lions, but also by the paws of the snow leopards. There are plenty of frighteningly huge cats out there. Why are we fucking with nature to make even bigger ones? In fact, if we're going to fuck with nature, why don't we try to breed snow leopards that don't get any bigger than house cats? Why don't we try to breed itty bitty lions? Picture a lion, with a full mane and everything, but no bigger than a bunny rabbit. Now *that* is something worth trying for.

"Holy crap," I said, looking at the picture of a liger standing on its hind legs with its front paws resting on a raised platform that must have been twelve feet high.

"Why do you have pictures of ligers on your phone?" Mike asked.

"Because they're just so big." Kelly smiled.

"Huh," said Mike.

I feigned mild interest but made a mental note to later read up on ligers.

"You guys want to float the river sometime this week?" Kelly asked.

"Yes!" I answered.

Mike looked surprised, clearly picturing my fun face and my death grip on the children.

"What?" I said. "It's fun, it's free, and I think it would be great for the girls to go one more time this summer."

"Well, I'm swamped, so I can't go. You sure you want to take the girls?"

"We'll be fine," I answered. "We'll be with Kelly."

"Have you taught your girls water safety?" Kelly asked Mike. "Do they know how to turn a pair of pants into a flotation device?" I looked at him with skepticism. "No, really," he continued. "Everyone should know this. You take them off and tie them, and they can save your life."

I pictured myself, bobbing in the ocean, gulping gallons of sea water while trying to remove a pair of blue jeans. That in itself would be impossible, so I pictured myself in yoga pants, which seemed more feasible. Even then, was I to tie the legs together and blow into the waist opening, trying to create a big yoga pants balloon that would keep me afloat until search and rescue arrived? And this was some sort of skill he wanted to teach my children?

"Kelly, our girls can't even button their own pants," I said.

"Okay, but I'm just saying. It's something everyone should know."

The day of our river float came, and I could tell that Mike was agitated. "Mike, we're going to be with Kelly," I reminded him. "We'll be just fine."

It was amazing to me that I was suddenly so relaxed with the idea, while Mike was now worried. But Mike will worry about any situation in which he is not present to do everything in his power to ensure the safety of his children.

"I'm not worried about you," Mike said. "I'm worried about all those annoying teenagers and twenty-somethings who should know better than to swing out on some stupid rope or jump off a bridge, not to mention they're completely inept at calculating when families are floating by. That bugs the shit out of me."

"Apparently so," I said. I refrained from admitting that I thought it was kind of fun watching the rope-swingers and bridge-jumpers.

In addition to Kelly's apparent ability to turn pants into a flotation device, he is a Master Diver and, by his own admission, more comfortable in the water than on land. "I'll be in the water, holding on to the boat the whole time," he assured us.

The only real problem with this plan was that Kelly had never floated the Boise River before. And perhaps I neglected to tell him about the shallow parts and falls. In any case, Kelly and I loaded up the girls and drove both our cars to the end of the river float, leaving one parked there. Then we piled in the other car and drove to the start. It was about eleven o'clock in the morning, and no one was there, which I found curious. After all, it was a gorgeous summer day.

Kelly's plan was to wear his wetsuit and stay mostly in the water, but rent an inner tube and tie it to our raft in case he needed to get out and rest at certain times. As we soon discovered, the reason no one was at the head of the river was because the raft and tube rental place didn't open until noon.

"Oh well," he said. "I guess I'll just stay in the water the whole time."

"And you can always climb in our raft if you need to," I said, though I doubted it. There was no way that Kelly would be able to fit in the raft with the girls and me. And even if he could, I could not picture any scenario in which Kelly could enter our raft from the water without tipping us over.

I would have objected to the idea of someone doing the whole trip in the water if it was anyone other than Kelly. The river float is about a three-hour trip. I'd known Kelly for over a decade and heard countless stories during those years of how Kelly's a Master Diver. Of how Kelly fashioned his own scuba gear at a ridiculously young age because he wanted to learn how to breathe underwater. Of how Kelly and another diving friend purposely sabotage each other's dive gear because they are so confident in their abilities in the water that they feel it's okay to toy with each other's oxygen supply. If Kelly was really such a fish, this would be his chance to prove it.

The trip was hard, not just because I didn't have Mike there to paddle so that I could keep the children held in my protective vice grip, but because having Kelly hanging on to the boat often rendered much of my paddling useless.

"You should see all the bull trout down here," he said when he surfaced. "I'll try and get a video." He returned to his snorkel and underwater camera and disappeared. He resurfaced a moment later and said, "I saw one this big." He held his hands apart, and I tried to look impressed, as if I had any idea what the average size of a bull trout was.

"Wow, that's great," I said. "Can you find me a paddle?" The paddle I used was borrowed from the neighbors, and I thought that Kelly scouring the bottom of the river would be a perfect opportunity to procure one of my own.

"Do you want any golf balls? There are a million golf balls down here."

"No, I want a paddle. Why would I want a golf ball? Find me a paddle." Eventually, he did find me a paddle, but the hours of swimming took a toll on Kelly, and he spent the last third of the trip gently hanging on to the back of the boat and trying not to die of exhaustion as I paddled us down the river. To keep from being a drag on the boat, he spent much of this time stretched straight out behind us with his head in the water, breathing through his snorkel. As a result, it appeared as if I was merrily rowing my two little girls down the river while dragging a body behind.

We passed under a bridge, and a group of men sat along the shore. They looked like they might be homeless, or alcoholic, or both, the type of people who hang out under bridges.

One of them hollered out to me, "What are you towing there?"

"A body," I answered confidently, and paddled on.

At the end of the float, I texted Mike to let him know that we were all alive and well. We deflated the raft, packed everything into Kelly's waiting truck, and drove back to the start of the float to retrieve mine. Kelly stopped by our house that evening to show off the video footage he'd taken, and I can now confidently state that a video of bull trout swimming could not possibly be more boring.

"Look at that one!" Kelly pointed to the screen.

"Yep," I said, unable to fake enthusiasm.

"Are you exhausted?" Mike asked him. "That's a long time to be in the water."

"Yes," he admitted. "Next time, I definitely need a tube. Especially for going over some of those shallow falls. They're uh… a little painful on the tender parts."

Personally, I have no desire to float the river in anything but a raft. Mike once floated the river in an inner tube for his brother Virgil's bachelor party. I expected him to finish the day excited, but he came home scowling.

"What's wrong?" I asked.

"Don't ever float the river in an inner tube."

"Why not?"

"It's one of those things that everyone did as a child and has fond memories of, but as an adult, it just sucks."

"Like running through sprinklers?"

"Exactly," he said.

"I get that part, but you seem downright bitter."

"Well, I kind of got separated from everyone else, so I just kind of did it alone, and it was all sort of lame."

"Oh."

"And I got separated from my own cooler."

Here he finally admitted the root of his dismay. This was back in the days when beer was still allowed on the river, before the powers that be realized that too many people who drink, drink too much. That's never a good combination with a body of water involved. Even worse than the potential health risks, river drinkers littered, junking up the banks with their discarded cans of PBR.

So Mike had set out that morning excited about floating the river in celebration of his brother's upcoming wedding, only to end up cold, alone, and stranded from his beer while Virgil and his bar buddies enjoyed themselves.

"Goodness sakes, I thought you had a great time," Virgil protested later when the subject came up.

"No, you and your friends had a great time," Mike said. "I wasn't even with you guys for most of the trip."

"Well, what the fuck, let's do it again," Virgil said.

"No," Mike blurted out. "No, really, that's okay."

Virgil's mood swings and general bipolar qualities are often evidenced like this in his speech. I don't know many people who will seamlessly use the terms "goodness sakes" and "what the fuck" within the same thirty seconds. But both are integral parts of his vocabulary.

There aren't many parts of Virgil's life that stay the same for very long. He's no longer married or in the army, for instance, both the military and his ex-wife having decided that he was too much to handle, after all. His relatives feel the same way. Sometimes I welcome his company, and at other times, just the thought of a conversation with Virgil makes me tired. But I'm pretty sure that Virgil and some of my other in-laws feel the same about me from time to time. I'm sure it's not easy to relax with me hovering nearby, clutching a giant tub of disinfecting wipes, ready to clean up whatever mess another person may cause.

Ironically, if I have to pick one person to help me clean up the kitchen after having the entire family over for dinner, that person is always Virgil. For all that he may reek like an ashtray, compelling me to make him stand still while I spray him from head to toe with Febreze, and for all his talk of various chafing body parts or how he likes to routinely smell his socks, Virgil is actually the only member of the Turner family who fully grasps both my need for clean and the correct way to get it. I suspect that other members of the family think I simply like things clean and orderly; they don't understand that I am *compelled* to make them so. It's not that I want to be a raging, compulsive bitch; it's that I *am* a raging, compulsive bitch.

And while other members of the family try to appease this side of me, they often go about it in a way that just inspires more panic in me. For instance, there is a difference between a paper towel and a cloth dish towel, and I feel I should conduct a class highlighting these differences and then create a test with various scenarios. Everyone will have to take the test and, in each scenario, choose whether the paper towel or the cloth towel is most suitable. For instance, if you are drying off clean hands, the correct answer would be the cloth towel. If you have inexplicably coated your hand in a condiment or sticky substance, which you would like to wipe off of yourself, the correct answer would be the paper towel. If you answer that a dish towel should be used both to dry clean dishes and to wipe the thick, gelatinous slime from raw chicken up off of my kitchen floor, then you are no longer allowed to enter my kitchen. Virgil gets these things, and for that I am thankful.

* * *

CHAPTER FOUR

Jersey Shore

"Welcome to *Aht* Camp!" She could have been straight out of *The Sopranos*. And of course, she was welcoming us to *Art* Camp. "I'm Miss Li*nnn*da." I assumed she held the *n* for an extended note in order to give us time to absorb the full meaning.

Miss Linda was incredibly loud. Her normal speaking voice was the level most Americans use when talking to foreigners, that illogical propensity for thinking more volume will equal greater understanding. I figured if Miss Linda ever spoke to a foreigner, she'd break their eardrums. Heavyset and in her late fifties, Miss Linda was caked with thick makeup, her fingers were capped with long, pink nails, and her head was topped off with platinum hair that had been fried to a crisp.

Art Camp took place in the classroom of an elementary school and was for children ages four, five, and six. We'd spent the previous two weeks telling three-year-old Ivy that despite the fact that she hadn't yet had her birthday party, she was, in fact, four. This was a lie.

I'm not a fan of lying. I'm not very good at it. When I lie, I stutter and sweat, my eyes shift nervously back and forth, and my skin grows inexplicably itchy. I do not possess a poker face. But in this case, lying to my child about her age so that she could attend Art Camp along with her older sister Emilia was preferable to the more terrifying scenario of spending all day, every day, with my children. Don't get me wrong, I love my children. They are the most awesome kids on the planet. But their ability to say the word "mom" four hundred times in five minutes makes me even itchier than lying.

When Art Camp ended, Ivy would return to the age of three, until her birthday, when she would again be four. This led to a bit of confusion for both of our children regarding the progression of time and age. I fear they will someday fail physics, and it will be all my fault. Actually, if they're working with my genes, they'll fail physics anyway, regardless of whether or not I toy with the space-time continuum.

I try not to abuse the power of being able to lie to my children and having them believe me. They are naïve and gullible and innocent, as children should be. They believe in the tooth fairy and Santa with all of their tiny might. Their conviction is so beautiful and pure that I want it to last for as long as possible. If I lie too much, they're sure to catch on, so I save it for really important situations, like Art Camp.

Miss Linda introduced us to Miss Terry, the other Art Camp teacher. She shared similarities with Miss Linda, though she was a little bit less in every way. Less bulky, less makeup, less loud. She was in her sixties and had dyed red hair that was a little less fried.

Mike and I walked Emilia and Ivy around the room, pointing out random objects with great enthusiasm. "Look, girls, *crayons!*" Mike exclaimed. This is the enthusiasm we employ when we're about to leave our kids in a new environment. We want them to feel incredibly lucky that we're letting them stay in a classroom that has the best crayons. Ever.

Miss Linda and Miss Terry began to hover in the way that care providers do when they want parents to leave. Their attentiveness acts as a polite means of saying, *Get the fuck out of here.* We kissed the girls goodbye, and they ran off to explore the room.

"Don't worry, they'll be just fine," said Miss Linda as she herded us to the door. She motioned to Miss Terry. "Her baby's a lawyer. And mine is forty-two."

It took me a minute to process this. Miss Linda put parents at ease with the rationale that it's okay to leave your children with someone if the caregiver has raised her own child to be a lawyer, or at least kept them alive until the age of forty-two. I wondered what the forty-two-year-old did for a living, and how he or she would feel about the fact that the best thing Mommy Linda could come up with to say about them was their age.

"Oh," Mike and I said in unison. We tried to sound impressed, sensing that both women were very proud of their respective lawyer and forty-two-year-old.

"Wow," said Mike under his breath as we left the school and made our way back to our borrowed beach house. "So, that's New Jersey."

"That's New Jersey," I confirmed.

We'd come to Jersey to live for a month, and while not all of the people we encountered fit this stereotype, there was no denying that we saw our fair share of gold chains, orange skin, and velour, often on the same person. The accent was thick in the Jersey air, which carried the scent of saltwater and deep-fried Twinkies.

New Jersey wasn't a place that occupied a coveted spot on our list of potential travel destinations, but someone had offered to rent our house in Idaho for a month. When someone threatens to hand over a few thousand dollars, we have a hard time saying no. We agreed to rent out our home, took the money, and worried after the fact about where we'd live during that month.

About the same time we took money from complete strangers who may or may not have had the intention of taking over our identities, which would doubtless end up as a made-for-TV movie and therefore be worth the hassle, I met one of my aunts for the first time. My mother has a slew of brothers and sisters I may never meet, all the children of an Irish Catholic couple who procreated with vigor but failed miserably when it came to caring for their children. My mother and her siblings were adopted into various households and lost touch over the years, until a handful of the clan reconnected in adulthood. When I first met my Aunt K live and in the flesh, we hit it off. When she heard of our dilemma over what to do for the month of July, she offered us her four-bedroom beach house in New Jersey as a remedy to our displacement.

Mike and I work on our laptops. We can work anywhere that has an Internet connection. We also love to travel, so we see no point in spending every day of the year working from the same place. We try to do as many extended trips as possible. The Jersey beach house seemed like the perfect situation, especially if the girls would be occupied with Art Camp for a few hours during the day. Mike and I could maintain the working adult thing and then hang out with our daughters at the beach in the afternoons.

When it was time to pick them up, I had the nervous anticipation every parent feels when retrieving your child after a first day.

"How did it go?" I asked the room at large when we arrived.

"Mommy! Mommy!" the girls chanted.

"It went okay," said Miss Linda, and the way she said okay indicated that it was not okay. "But some of us need to work on our manners a little bit." Her eyes darted to Emilia.

"What happened?" I asked.

"Little Miss didn't want to do what the rest of the group was doing," she said. And the way she referred to my daughter as Little Miss made it clear that she'd singled Emilia out on day one as the troublemaker.

Emilia cowered behind me.

"Okay, we'll talk about it," I assured Miss Linda.

As the four of us walked home, Mike asked, "What happened, Emilia?"

"I just didn't want to watch the movie," she said, with her head hanging.

"Movie?" I asked. "You watched a movie?"

"Yes," said Emilia. "And it was scary and there was a plant and it was alive and it ate the boy and I didn't like it."

"*I* wasn't scared," Ivy piped up, "because I'm four years old."

"Well, I'm six years old, and I *was* scared," Emilia moped.

"What about art?" Mike demanded. "Did you do any art projects at Art Camp?"

"I think so, but I can't remember," said Emilia.

"We had cookies!" added Ivy.

If we wanted our kids to watch movies and eat cookies, they could certainly do so in our care. We wouldn't have to pay someone sixty dollars to press play, and we could select something that wouldn't induce nightmares. In front of our children, however, we hid our frustrations with Art Camp, specifically because we sensed that our new environment had Ivy on edge. It required only a miniscule amount of negativity to set Ivy off on a tantrum or tirade. This was a dangerous state that was always heightened during a walk, when we were outside and vulnerable to the condemnation of the general public. She could make or break any adventure. And every parent knows that while you don't want your three-year-old to control the family dynamics, sometimes you tread lightly just to make it through the day. This was one of those days.

When we dropped the kids off at Art Camp the following morning, it appeared that the other attendees who'd already arrived were unsupervised on the playground. This was another thing I didn't want to pay for. We were perfectly capable of failing to supervise our own children. *But surely there's an inept attendant lurking in a corner somewhere,* I told myself. I entered the classroom and approached Miss Linda.

"So... I had a question about yesterday," I said.

"What's the problem?" She narrowed her eyes and held her hands up in a defensive gesture, as if she could tell that

I was going to be a troublemaker, just like my ill-mannered children.

"Did they watch something? Emilia's been talking nonstop about a movie they watched that really scared her."

"Oh, that," she said. "Yeah, the boys were watching *Goosebumps*. And if it were up to me, they wouldn't watch anything." This was what I wanted to hear, that she didn't want the children to watch anything; this was supposed to be Art Camp. But I didn't get the part about it not being up to her. Were the six-year-old boys actually in charge? Was this like one of those alternative schools where the kids determined the curriculum? If that was the case, why wasn't it included in the brochure? She continued, "In fact, I told them just to bring in their video games." She pantomimed holding an electronic device and pushing buttons furiously with her thumbs.

"Okay." I nodded, as if this all made sense. There were so many things wrong with what she'd just said, I didn't know how to respond. She'd shown the four- to six-year-olds (okay, three- to six-year-olds) a movie designed to scare tweens. What went on in Art Camp was apparently not up to her, the teacher. And she encouraged attendees to bring their video games. Maybe video games were a better option to her because they wouldn't require any effort on her part. With movies, she had to put the cassette into the VCR and press play. Because surely none of those kids knew how to work a VCR, which was the classroom's audio/visual component. The children probably dealt in DVDs and Netflix and Hulu, or other, newer, better things that I haven't learned about yet, but that my children will someday teach me. With the children bringing their own video games, Miss Linda could relinquish her VCR responsibilities and would be free to do even less than whatever it was she already did.

As Mike and I walked back to the house after dropping the girls off for day two, he said, "I'm not digging Art Camp."

"I know."

"It would've been cheaper just to get a babysitter for a few hours here and there."

"I know."

"I think we should cancel it."

"We've paid for the week. Let's just finish it out."

He grumbled on about Art Camp as we entered the house and fired up our laptops to get started on the workday. The doorbell rang. He shot me a look that told me he had no intention of opening the door and would be perfectly content to hide inside the house and pretend that we were not, in fact, there. Seizing the opportunity to be a better person, I answered the door.

"Hi there, I live just three doors down. I'm Mickey." A tiny woman with gray hair and glasses stood on the step.

"I'm Amanda," I said. I started to extend my hand for a shake but decided that somehow that would be an awkward interaction. She looked relieved.

"How long are you here for?" she asked. "Are you renting?"

"Actually, this is my aunt's place, and we're here for about a month."

She seemed giddy and desperate for friendly neighbors.

"I saw you walking with your girls. Have you been to Ocean City yet?"

"We haven't," I said. "We actually don't have a car, so we just stick around the neighborhood or head to the beach."

This news excited her further. "Well, we were thinking about going to Ocean City this afternoon. Would you like to come?"

In essence, this old lady was asking my family out on a date.

"Oh, that sounds like fun," I said, though I was terrified at the prospect of spending an afternoon with someone I didn't know. What if she was crazy? Or worse, boring? "The girls are at Art Camp until one o'clock, but we might be able to join you after that. I'll need to talk to my husband." I said this as if he wasn't actually there, sitting just around the corner from where I stood. I could feel gratitude radiating from him, a silent thanks for giving him a free pass on the conversation.

"Okay, here's our number." She handed me a slip of paper that read *Mickey and Marty* with a phone number underneath. "You talk to your husband and then give me a call." She smiled at me and offered a little wave before walking down the steps and toward her house.

When I closed the door, Mike let out a loud groan from the other room.

"What?" I demanded. "It could be fun." I had no idea how many opportunities for activities we'd have. It seemed wrong to turn it down outright, even if she did turn out to be crazy.

"Or it could be awful."

"I think we should go."

He groaned again.

My phone rang, and it was a call I'd been waiting for. I picked it up and took it out to the front porch so I wouldn't be a distraction to Mike. It was an important call, at least to me, a business call with a publisher. As I began speaking, a car slowed right in front of the house. For a second I thought I was going to be the victim of a drive-by shooting. Two female heads craned from inside the car, leaning toward and out the driver's side window. They were normal-sized humans, but everything except for their bodies seemed exaggerated and huge. They had big hair, oversized sunglasses, and hoop earrings the size of oranges. I was still trying to carry on my phone conversation but couldn't help looking at them since they were looking at me. If they needed directions, I hoped they'd stop to ask someone who wasn't obviously on the phone. But they stayed and stared, until the driver called loudly, "I grew up in that house!" Then she added, "We both did!" and pointed back and forth between herself and—apparently— her sister, seated in the passenger seat. Could they not see that I was on the phone? I pointed to the phone as evidence and simultaneously started babbling incoherently to the publisher on the other end of the line. Would he still want to publish my writing now that he was learning I could barely form a sentence? It was one of those awkward moments when multi- tasking is impossible, when it becomes clear that attempting to do two things at once will yield failure at both.

It is physically and mentally impossible to carry on two conversations at once. I struggle as it is when confronted with more than one auditory stimulus. When we are at home and have music playing, Mike will walk over to the couch, sit, and turn on the television. My brain instantly muddles, my ears unable to focus on more than one input at the same time. I lunge for the music to silence it before my head explodes, and before one of my children approaches me with yet a further demand on my attention, invariably a question involving why

George Washington had to die and how Emilia really misses him, or Ivy requesting we play Baby Lions, in which we all pretend to be baby lions.

But I was caught on the step in the middle of the phone conversation while also being yelled at by two women in a car. I could not turn them off, nor could I bring myself to end the important phone call with the publisher. Still, the women sat and stared at me expectantly, as if waiting for me to invite them in for a tour and a wine cooler.

"I'm on the phone," I called out to them. They smiled and stared at me for a moment longer before finally relenting and driving on.

I finished my call just as dark clouds rolled in and rain-drops began to fall. I walked back inside the house and said to Mike, "It's raining."

He looked up at me and smiled. "Does that mean we can't go to Ocean City with Minnie?"

"Mickey," I corrected. "And yes, we're probably off the hook."

I located Mickey and Marty's phone number and dialed.

"Hello?" answered the hoarse voice of a man.

"Hello, this is Amanda. I live just a few doors down."

"Yeah?"

"Mickey had mentioned going to Ocean City this after—"

"Hey, Mickey," he cut me off and called to his wife. I jerked the phone from my ear, startled. "It's a girl down the street. *You* talk to her."

"Hello?" came the sweet voice of Mickey.

"It's Amanda," I said. "It looks like the weather is turning on us."

"Yes," she agreed. "Perhaps we'll have to go another time."

"Okay, well thanks for the invite," I said and hung up, grateful that I'd learned that Marty was a rude asshole before committing my family to an entire outing with him and his, no doubt, long-suffering wife.

When it was time to pick up the girls from Art Camp, Mike and I located umbrellas and set out in the rain. In the classroom, I noticed for the first time that an entire wall was lined with VHS movies, and a huge plastic tub of cheese puffs sat on a nearby table. We limited our interactions with Miss Linda and Miss Terry and on the way home asked the kids how their day was.

"Good," said Ivy. "We had cookies."

"Did you watch a movie?" I asked.

"Yes," answered Emilia. "Today it was *Harry Potter.*"

I'm a *Harry Potter* fan, myself. But there are plenty of moments in the *Harry Potter* movies that could easily scare the crap out of a six-year-old, much less a three-year-old pretending to be four.

"Were you scared?"

"No," they answered together.

"Harry Potter?" said Mike in shock. "Those movies are like three hours long. Art Camp is only four hours. This is ridiculous."

The ridiculousness lasted for a total of four days. We'd paid for one week, and Art Camp was cancelled on Friday for the Fourth of July weekend. When Thursday afternoon rolled around and we picked up the girls, eager to learn which movie they'd watched and how much high-fructose corn syrup with lard they'd consumed, we discovered that they'd painted pictures, ostensibly so that the teachers could, in fact, claim that they were conducting an Art Camp.

"These aren't dry yet, honey," Miss Linda said to Ivy.

"You'll have to wait and pick it up on Monday," added Miss Terry.

"Okay, that's fine," I said. "Girls, say goodbye," I instructed.

They dutifully did so.

"We'll see you Monday," Miss Linda called, waving her long pink nails in the air.

And I couldn't help but mutter, "Like hell you will."

* * *

CHAPTER FIVE

Curb Your Dog

"We don't need camp, anyway," I reasoned.

"Yes," agreed Mike. "The girls are old enough to play together. And our movie selection isn't nearly as scary."

"All right, but if we're going to ask them to play and allow us time to work, we have to do some sort of activity with them first. Otherwise they're never going to leave us alone."

I'm not exactly sure what I had in mind as far as activities go. I just knew that I'd feel like a complete screw-up as a mother if I woke, put a movie on, and went straight for my computer. I wanted to have some sort of interaction with them so that when I did turn a movie on, my guilt would be less.

When you're about to become a parent for the first time, no one ever mentions, in all of their advice, that a huge part of parenting is managing your guilt. The range of things for which parents are made to feel guilty is overwhelming, and it requires complex scheduling to make sure you feel sufficiently guilty for all of your shortcomings. These may include but are not limited to what they eat, what they watch, what they wear, the amount of time you spend with them, your lack of patience, and the fact that Candyland is only bearable with a drink nearby.

I also thought it would be good for us to get outside, maybe do something healthy. We needed physical activity to counteract the fact that both Mike and I spend hours every day sitting on our asses. I hope one day to buy a treadmill desk, because being able to walk and work at the same time seems like the best multitasking idea ever, and then at the end of the day I could pour myself an enormous vat of wine, sit on the couch, and watch *Wipe-Out* reruns with my kids and not let the encroaching feelings of slothfulness overtake me entirely.

When I do get my treadmill desk, I'm going high-end. I'm not messing around with a cheap version that will rattle and make me feel like a moron for my inability to assemble it. I'm going to drop thousands of dollars, and the fat will melt off my body while I write romances bordering on porn under a fake name. But that's all in the future. For the time being, I just needed some daily activity, not only to keep my butt from further expanding and to avoid having people ask me when I was due, but also because we spent most afternoons at the beach. Our beach posture mirrors our working posture, which is to say that it's another setting in which we sit on our ever-widening asses.

The beach house was a block and a half from the board-walk. *Maybe we'll take walks together*, I thought. But then I remembered how difficult it was to get my children to walk to and from Art Camp. They complain after roughly forty seconds of walking, with grievances of "My feet hurt" and the endless question of "Are we there yet?" They are simply not fun to walk with, especially in light of the fact that a three-year-old's temperament often seems far more hormonal than it could possibly be at that age, unless you're moving toward a goal that somehow involves sugar. If we head to an ice-cream parlor, for example, they walk happily for miles.

Aunt K had bikes in the garage of the house she was lending us, and I sensed that my decade-long avoidance of the bicycle had come to an end. I was going to have to get back in the saddle. The excuse of "I've forgotten how" wasn't going to work, because somebody somewhere once said that you never forget how to ride a bike. I bet if I tried really hard, I could forget, or at least fake it.

"Come on," Mike said. "This is the perfect place to start riding a bike again."

"Fine," I relented.

I wasn't always inept on a bike, and I remember hours spent riding around the neighborhood when I was a child. I even remember my bike's name and how my sister laughed at it. It wasn't a name that came with the bike, but a name I bestowed on the bike.

"Golden Blue," I told her, hearing for the first time the ridiculous twang in my voice as I said it.

"You named your bike Golden Blue?" she said.

By then I wanted to change my mind, but it was too late. "Yes," I asserted with my chin in the air, wishing I'd kept the name a secret. A secret that only Golden Blue and I would share.

At some point in early adulthood, I lost my athleticism and bravery. I couldn't get enough of newspaper stories of death and tragedy in the world and consumed these like other women buy shoes or read romance novels. The endless articles I read on the deaths of cyclists, combined with a newfound love of tobacco and a suffocating fear of embarrassing myself in front of others, created a perfect storm to separate me completely from any biking activities.

I'd made it through my twenties, given up cigarettes, and learned that I was capable of embarrassing myself regardless of my mode of transport. I might as well stop being such a grump and give it a shot.

The idea of riding on the boardwalk was at least less terrifying than the thought of riding in traffic, where I'd surely lose control of my bike and ride straight into an oncoming U-Haul. That's just not how I want to die. I think more than the terror I feel when riding a bike, must be the fear a bystander feels when they see me mounting a bike in proximity to them. When I start, I wobble precariously back and forth, my front wheel swinging wildly from side to side as I try not to fall over, until I can get some momentum to help me stabilize. Part of why I'm so wobbly in the beginning is that I am unable to start with my left foot. So if the pedals are in any position other than the right foot ready to press down, I jerkily hop along until I'm in that position. Surely I can't be the only person who suffers from a deficiency in their left limb coordination. Did I have a stroke at some point without realizing it? And will it develop into future issues? Will I wake one day with the inability to turn left? Will that mean my level of intelligence is on par with that of Derek Zoolander? Nevertheless, I managed to ride a bike regularly along the boardwalk, always beginning by discreetly walking the bike along until the right pedal was in starting position.

I was grateful for all of the rules and regulations on the East Coast. These involved not permitting bikes on the boardwalk past ten in the morning, because the crowds were simply too thick and bikes became a hazard. This meant that if I had to ride a bike, at least the powers that be had instituted rules that would get me out of having to ride a bike all day.

Mike went online and found a used bike trailer with which we could tow the kids. We adopted a morning routine of setting out on the bikes, taking along coffee, milk, bagels, and cream cheese. We'd ride a few miles and then sit and have a picnic while people-watching or staring at the ocean. One morning, we decided to skip the picnic and instead rode to Atlantic City, where we took the girls to a diner on the boardwalk. We drank milkshakes for breakfast, telling ourselves that milkshakes contain milk and are therefore entirely appropriate as a first meal of the day. We paid no attention to the time.

"Amanda," Mike said as we exited the diner and returned to our bikes. "It's after ten o'clock."

"Okay," I said. "We'll just walk the bikes back."

The girls climbed into the bike trailer, and Mike and I began walking the bikes back toward Ventnor City.

"Mom," Ivy whined. "Why are we going so slow?"

"Yeah, why aren't you and Daddy riding the bikes?" Emilia asked. "This is taking *forever*."

Another thing that people don't warn you about in terms of having children is that kids learn to roll their eyes and sound entirely annoyed with their parents long before the teenage years. I'd thought that the ability to make the word "forever" sound like a horribly unbearable grievance wouldn't start until at least the age of thirteen. Much to my dismay, both of my girls learned to sound exasperated and annoyed by the age of three.

"Bikes aren't allowed on the boardwalk right now, girls," Mike explained.

"And you two still get to ride," I reasoned, "so why are you complaining? Daddy and I are the ones that have to do all the work."

And work we did. I hadn't realized quite how far we'd traveled. As we marched our bikes back along the boardwalk and I silently thought to myself, *This is taking forever,* a cop in a golf cart pulled up alongside us.

"Are you two done for the day?" he asked.

"Are we... uh...?" I didn't understand the question. Done with what? Had he been following us? Were we under surveillance for something? Would we be on a special New Jersey season of *COPS?*

"Are you heading back for the day?" he asked, as if this made it clear. Back where? How did he know from where we'd originated? Had he mistaken us for another family?

"We're heading back to Ventnor City," I said.

"And you're walking..."

"Yes," I confirmed. "We are walking." With each exchange, I felt we were drifting further apart from any possible understanding.

"*Why* are you walking?" he asked. He started to sound as annoyed with me as my children, and I was afraid he'd assume I was on drugs, as opposed to just stupid, and would pepper spray me.

"Because we thought we weren't allowed to ride our bikes." I looked at my wrist, as if to indicate we were in a bike-free time of day.

"Go ahead and ride your bikes," he said. "If anyone says anything, you tell them Officer Ritchie told you that you could ride home."

The policeman and I were two intelligent people trying to communicate, but the differences between New Jersey and Idaho created an extra level of fog we had to get through before we could understand each other. I realized then that we weren't under surveillance or in danger of pepper spray. He was trying to show us some mercy, letting us bend the rules because the sun was growing hot and we were towing two kids.

"Okay, thanks." We smiled and waved as he puttered on down the boardwalk.

Mike and I stopped and looked at each other.

"You don't want to ride, do you?" he asked.

"Well... it's just..."

Being given a free pass is one thing, but other people wouldn't know we'd been given a free pass, so it still felt wrong, or like I was asking for trouble. Surely, the native Jerseyans would begin flinging Coney dogs and bottles of suntan oil at us. And what if another cop stopped us? Would anyone else give a shit what Officer Ritchie said? Was this a power struggle and pissing match between various members of the golf cart law-enforcement brigade? What if Officer Ritchie rode back in our direction, only to see that we continued to walk despite his kind offer? Then it would be like we'd directly disobeyed the orders of a police officer. We'd end up in a Jersey jail, and our children would be taken by the state and then farmed out to families that would shun them for being blonde, force them to use tanning beds, and raise them to speak with an abundance of slang. It was a lose-lose situation.

"Mom, I want to go in there!" Emilia said, pointing to the bright lights of a casino.

"I'm sorry, sweetie, but that's a casino, and kids aren't allowed in casinos."

"Why not?"

"Because they gamble in there. And gambling is something that's only allowed for adults, like alcohol."

"If kids aren't allowed in there," she said, "then why do they make it look like a really fun place for kids to go?"

"I'm not sure, sweetie. Either because they want to attract the child-like minds or because they really want you to want to go there when you grow up."

"Huh?"

"Never mind. Maybe later today we'll go to the beach!" I said to distract her.

"Awesome!"

We settled into New Jersey easily. Riding bikes in the morning, working for most of the day, and then spending afternoons at the beach with the girls. We flew kites, jumped waves, and became regulars at the local library. Our explorations of the shops along the Atlantic City boardwalk were limited, as I found their combinations of wares disturbing. But who am I to judge? Maybe there really is a demand for a souvenir shop that also sells baby clothes, stuffed animals, bongs, and frighteningly realistic toy AK-47s.

No matter how many afternoons we spent at the beach, it was never dull. Emilia could often be found at the shoreline in an obscene, wide-stance squat, trying to free the crotch of her swimsuit from the pound of sand that had accumulated there. Or she'd scour the beach for shells and then try to sell them for a dollar a piece to the other beachgoers. Not wanting to stifle her entrepreneurial spirit, I convinced her to take the shells back to the house, paint them, and then try to sell them. Still, she never made a sale.

Ivy spent much of her time at the beach hiding in the shade under the boardwalk. The upside of this, I convinced myself, was that at least she wasn't under there doing drugs or making out with a transient. Her location was also a nice safe distance from the water, which allowed us to breathe a little easier. When either of our kids approached the water, we kept a close watch, not just out of basic parental instinct, but also because while some of the lifeguards were very attentive, others were only attentive to their iPhones or focused on flexing for passing girls. The end of every beach visit involved a complex twenty-step process to clean everyone up without dragging the entire beach, most of which was located in the crotch of Emilia's swimsuit, into Aunt K's home.

We were ecstatic when Aunt K came for a visit, and I scrubbed every inch of the house in preparation, hoping she'd feel we were immaculate and considerate guests and therefore offer us free use of her beach house every year. But Aunt K was not alone. She showed up with Chico, a small, black, pug-like dog with a lot of energy. He was very nice. He was too nice. Ivy's fear of dogs reduced her to tears, while Chico couldn't understand why she wouldn't play with him. In addition, Ivy had a minor allergic reaction to Chico, something that occurs with her and certain dogs, but not all dogs. When she has this reaction, her right eye puffs up until she looks like she's been abused, both eyes tear without end, which makes her look like she's bawling, no doubt from all the abuse she's suffered, and her nose becomes itchy and sneezy. Ivy's complete and utter rejection of Chico must have seemed like a slap in the face to Aunt K. We installed a baby gate at the top of the stairs, and Ivy watched *Hercules* over and over in our bedroom while Chico remained downstairs. I've always found Ivy's obsession with *Hercules* peculiar. It's not the worst animated movie I've seen, but even the most hardcore Danny DeVito fans might object to repeatedly watching him in a role where he is half-goat and sings a solo. Not that I'm one to judge. I have a voice for print. In any case, the situation was not ideal.

There is only one dog that Ivy is not afraid of, and that is my in-laws' dog, Sitka. Part of what allayed her fear with Sitka was that we would let Ivy walk him, and in this manner, she gradually became comfortable with him. We thought we'd try the same thing with Chico, but Chico's energy and enthusiasm prohibited Ivy from ever really warming up to him.

On our many attempts to walk with Ivy and Chico throughout the neighborhood, I noticed an abundance of signs reading: Curb your dog. This is not a common phrase in Idaho, and as someone who only thinks of a horrific scene from *American History X* when presented with the idea of curbing a living thing, I was a bit taken aback when I first saw it. While this won't come as news to natives of New Jersey, or perhaps even the greater East Coast, I feel the need to explain the message to the west. To curb your dog means to force your dog to poop on the curb, whether or not there is a strip of grass there. Other signs, some with unfortunate accompanying graphics, declare lawns "No Poop Zones." Residents don't want your dog pooping on their grass, even if you're going to clean up after your pet. This seems a bit ridiculous to me, because the only reason we have grass is so that lawn mower companies can continue to make lawn mowers and so that dogs have a place to crap. And I think having a sign staked in your yard with an outline of a dog taking a shit is actually worse than an actual shit. But that's just my personal preference. I'm a firm believer in poop-scooping, and there wouldn't be a need for such signs if pet owners would just take the twenty seconds needed to do it. There will always be the pet owner who will pretend, against all blatant logic, that he does not notice his dog crapping two feet from where he stands.

Between the "Curb your dog" campaign and the pristine beaches that were groomed every morning, it occurred to me that the East Coast is perhaps unnecessarily consumed with cleanliness. Not that I didn't appreciate the daily and meticulous grooming of the beach. And then I thought about my inability to leave crumbs on the counter, dishes in the sink, or a bed unmade, and I realized where my compulsions come from. I'm an East Coaster. I was born and raised in Maryland, and my mother is obsessive about cleaning, as is my Aunt K. It's in my blood, in my roots. My DNA cries out for sterility!

My husband and in-laws are from Alaska, which is about as far away from Maryland as you can get, in terms of the U.S. They are also about as far away from my compulsive cleaning as you can get, in terms of behavior. Even though I thought the dog-curbing was over the top, in a way, New Jersey felt like the well-ordered, anal-retentive home of my dreams.

Of course, the sterile nature of our surroundings only extended so far. Any hankering for the grubbier and seedier side of life was a mere ten-minute drive to Atlantic City.

Aunt K came for one last visit when our trip came to an end. I again scrubbed the house in preparation for her arrival, again wanting her to think that we were immaculate guests so that we might be invited back. To my dismay, I realized that we were anything but immaculate.

"So, just a few things about the place I wanted to point out," I said.

"Okay," she answered cautiously.

"We broke your coffee grinder. And there's a pen mark on the chair. And there's a wine stain on the rug upstairs, but I scrubbed it a lot, and really it almost came out. And there's a wine stain on the bedside table, and that one, I really couldn't get out. And maybe just a teeny drop of red wine on the bedspread. And we broke three of these glasses. Well, we didn't actually break them, I just realized too late that they can't go in the dishwasher, and so they cracked and, well, that's how the wine stain got on the bedside table. You see, we didn't really spill it, we just didn't realize the glass had a crack in it, and it sat there and must have leaked through."

"Okay," Auntie K said again. "Don't worry about it. I'm not worried about it."

"But that's not all."

"Oh."

"We also kind of destroyed all of your towels. Actually, it was me. I think I destroyed all of your towels." I led her to the bathroom and showed her that all of her towels, all of her fluffy, expensive towels, had bleach-like stains on them. This had to be my fault, because I have faulty skin. Surely the damage to the towels was caused by one of the various medications I apply to different parts of my skin in order to keep eczema, psoriasis, acne, and an unfortunate nail fungus under control.

"Hey," she said. "I'll buy new ones."

Despite the fact that Aunt K and I had met only recently, I detected early on that we share many similar traits. One of which is that we worship order and cleanliness and organization and all things neat and tidy. I'd felt that after our month in her home, we'd ruined it.

"Oh god, I'm so sorry," I said.

"No really," she assured me. "It's all fine. None of it's a big deal."

I smiled, thankful that she wasn't upset. And if she was upset, I'm thankful that she had the decency to lie about it.

After a month on the East Coast, visiting relatives and playing house in someone else's house, we traveled back to Boise. It occurred to me then that Idaho and New Jersey tend to look down on each other. When we told our fellow Idahoans that we went to New Jersey for a month, they all said, "Ugh, New Jersey? Why?" New Jerseyans should not be offended by this. Because parts of New Jersey are wonderful, and they should keep them as closely guarded secrets. So what if *Jersey Shore* has tainted how people feel about the Jersey Shore? Those of us who have been there know how wonderful it really is. In parts.

In New Jersey, whenever we told people we were from Idaho, they responded with, "Ugh, Idaho? What's in Idaho?

Potatoes?" Now sure, I concede that we have potatoes in Idaho. We have potato-shaped candy. We have potatoes on our license plates. And it's not just a potato; it's a baked potato, split down the middle with a big pat of butter melting in the center. I understand why the license plate designer people, who have really awesome jobs, went with the baked potato. Whenever someone uses a plain potato as a mascot or in a children's book, it ends up looking like a big shit, and that's unfortunate.

Yes, we are proud of our potatoes, but Idaho has so much more to offer. We're not all good ol' boys, and we don't all have gun racks. Many do, but many don't. When I first moved here, I called it White-a-ho and was dismayed at the overall lack of diversity. I didn't want my children to grow up having never been exposed to anyone who wasn't white. But Boise has since emerged as a big destination for refugees, and now we have an entire rainbow of people. Some might not think that diversity is a good thing, but I don't want to live next to those people anyway.

We returned to Boise, land of refugees, potatoes, and crap-friendly lawns, and to our home that's full of ruined towels but ironically and shockingly free of red wine stains.

* * *

CHAPTER SIX

That's Not a Balloon

"You are *not* going to believe this," I hissed into the phone.

"What?" said Mike.

"I think our renters had a dog," I said. "I can't believe they would do that. Our house is specifically listed as *no pets.*"

"What makes you think they had a dog?" he asked.

"Well, my first clue was the plastic bag left by the front door. The only people who keep plastic bags by the front door are people who need to clean up after their dogs."

"Okay, but a plastic bag doesn't mean anything. Is there fur?"

"No, not really. But I found dog food on the floor in the hall closet."

"Maybe they like dog food."

"They do not like dog food. They were liars, and they rented our house and brought a dog in here even though they knew it was specifically against the rules."

"Calm down, rule follower. Is there any damage?"

"No," I admitted. "I just can't believe someone would do that."

I continued cleaning the house from top to bottom, bitter at our dishonest tenants, bitter at the fact that I hadn't used their cleaning deposit to hire someone else to clean the house, and debating whether or not I would say something to them via email. Or even withhold some of their damage deposit that I was supposed to refund. Not that I could claim I needed the funds for repairs of any kind, but still, I felt that there should be a financial penalty just for breaking the rules.

Mike was correct; I'm a ridiculous rule follower. It's not just that I follow the rules because I don't want to get in trouble; I want others to get in trouble when they don't follow the rules. Because otherwise, why the fuck am I following all these rules?

When Mike came home that evening, I was still fuming.

"Why are you so tense?" he asked.

"I just can't believe they brought a dog in here," I said. "I mean, what if Ivy had an allergic reaction to our house because someone lived here for a month with an illegal animal."

"Did she have a reaction?"

"No, but she could have."

"But she didn't."

"Dogs are not allowed."

"Are you sure we didn't make some exception for them? Didn't they ask us about a dog at some point?"

I didn't remember much of our dealings with the tenants when they'd first asked to rent the house, because it had happened so long ago, but I was sure that no such exception had been made.

"I made up the contract," I insisted. "I promise you that it clearly states that no pets are allowed."

That was the first seed of doubt. I would seethe for two full days before finally pulling up the contract, which included the paragraph that usually stated that pets are not allowed, but which I had changed to read: *Pets are permitted and limited to the tenants' one small dog.*

"I am an asshole," I said to the computer screen when I read it. "Thank god I didn't yell at them for bringing their dog." And I hadn't really been upset about the dog, just about the sneakiness of it all, which turned out to be completely fabricated. Because of this incident, I no longer trust myself. Ever. I'm not yet forty but apparently block out entire conversations and legal, binding documents. This does not bode well for my golden years.

After I put the house back in order, we reacquainted with Boise and planned Ivy's birthday party. Since Art Camp was mercifully a thing of the past, we ceased lying to our child and admitted to her that she was, in fact, still three.

"We're going to have a party," I said, "and this time you're going to turn four, for real."

"Okay," she said, "but I'm going to keep my eye on you."

We had the birthday party at home and decided to forgo renting a jumpy house or playing games, like updated versions of Pin the Tail on the Donkey, which no longer involve actual pins, but usually just tape, and are more like Pin the Lips on the Frog. If you win, you've kissed the frog, and maybe it will turn into a prince, because somehow we still have a culture that tells little girls that all of their dreams will come true if they can just find their prince. I didn't want to do any more stupid games like those. There was always a kid or two who cheated and peeked, thereby assaulting my rule-following nature, so I instead hired professional entertainment. I paid for an hour of time from someone who made balloon animals and did face painting. But this particular professional took her arts to new levels. Instead of making balloon dogs and swords, she made balloon backpacks and birthday crowns. She made a balloon chainsaw and a working balloon bow and arrow. Then she made a little balloon apple that a kid could place on his head, while another kid used the balloon bow and the balloon arrow to shoot it. It made violent play between children positively darling. The kids were completely entertained, it was by someone other than me, and all for less than a hundred bucks. I should have stopped there.

Ivy is obsessed with all things sugar, so we had a birthday cake *and* an ice-cream-sundae bar. After choosing their ice cream of choice, the children ran down the length of our dining room table topping it off with chocolate chips, gummy bears, sprinkles, whipped cream, maraschino cherries, and syrups of the chocolate, caramel, and strawberry varieties. Perhaps this was a little much, as the desserts were followed by massive vomiting on the part of one of the four-year-old attendees. I'm not talking typical kid vomiting, but one of those impossible vomiting experiences where a small child appears to vomit the equivalent of three times his own body mass. The resulting eruption covered the walls of our hallway and an entire bathroom. Not only did the afflicted child live, but he didn't shed a tear. I felt like I should have had some sort of award on hand to present to him.

In addition to our daughters having fun with neighborhood playmates, the birthday party was a good opportunity for the family to get together and reconnect after our Jersey trip. I married into a family of startlingly good relationships in which no one secretly or not-so-secretly despises another family member. On the whole, my husband has a good relationship with his siblings. Sandi is the oldest and the shortest, a politically incorrect but well-intentioned dynamo with endless energy, enviable drive, and horrific organizational skills, which are, of course, made worse by her endless hoarding of clothes and shoes. Virgil (born Robert) is the middle child, the eccentric black sheep of the family who legally changed his name to Virgil. He has endless unbelievable stories that often, against all logic and expectations, somehow turn out to be true, and he is the only person I've ever known to gain weight at boot camp. The only explanation I can think of for how he managed this is that boot camp denied him his usual vices. Without nicotine and alcohol, Virgil turned to the only thing he was permitted to overdose on, which was food. He'd gorge himself on pancakes, bacon, and eggs every morning, and despite the physical demands of the army, he somehow managed to come home chubby. Perhaps because of the extra weight, he experienced some unfortunate chafing and would often write to me and request various powders, salves, and ointments. I didn't ask for details and instead sent him boxes of what I hoped would offer him some measure of relief, in order to avoid any further details of his chafing issues.

Mike is the youngest and a polar opposite of his brother, with a head for business and an appearance that would indicate he's a good little Mormon boy, while Virgil looks like a bastard child born of a Hell's Angels dating service. All three siblings seem to get along. I like my husband's siblings and try to make sure we all get together fairly regularly, not just on holidays and for birthdays, but also just for dinner or outings, because we all generally enjoy one another's company.

I texted Virgil: Taking girls to Hyde Park Street Fair. Want to come?

Virgil: Can't. Working. Worked till 2am last night. No one will help me on this job. Must get it done.

Virgil works in construction and remodeling. He can build, tile, paint, and is very good at what he does. But he won't do anything without firmly holding on to his right to complain about it every step of the way. I refused to take the bait of asking him more about the job.

Me: Come over for dinner some night this week.

Virgil: K.

The Hyde Park Street Fair is something I look forward to every year. Mike was working, but my mother-in-law offered to go with us. Before we set out, I painted the girls' faces. I have a little bit of artistic talent in me, the equivalent of an immensely gifted fifth grader. As I child, I wanted to be an artist, and I was encouraged by teachers who recognized my talent. That is, until about the sixth grade. The other artistic kids continued to develop their skills, while mine failed to thrive and remained, to this day, the equivalent of an immensely gifted fifth grader. Nevertheless, I often employ my stunted skills to paint my daughters' faces, rather than stand in line for an hour and pay someone else five dollars to do it.

"You're going to paint our faces!" Emilia exclaimed. "This is the best day of my whole life!"

My children are still at the delightfully innocent age where the slightest thing can cause a day to be the best day of their whole lives. So we have a lot of best days of our whole lives.

When Emilia's face was painted with butterflies in a rainbow of colors and Ivy had a cat face, which she punctuated with a headband and cat ears on her head, we headed to the Hyde Park Street Fair, along with my mother-in-law.

Of course, my preference would always be to attend this sort of event with my husband. We're lucky in that, after fourteen years of marriage, we still enjoy each other's company. In fact, we probably like each other more now than we did when we first got married. But there is one silver lining to going to a fair or festival without Mike, and that is that I have the opportunity to stuff my face with whatever type of horrible fair food I like and not feel any type of judgment.

For some reason, Mike and I feel embarrassed when eating unhealthy food in front of each other. Maybe that sounds ridiculous, but I think it's a good thing, because most of the time we are in each other's company, and therefore, most of the time we eat under the scrutiny of a spouse. This may sound tyrannical, but it's a two-way street and helps each of us keep the obese alter ego within from clawing its way out and into reality. But on the occasion when Mike is not with me and I'm presented with fair food, I'm going to order what I want to order. I feel like it's the reward I deserve for carting the children around to games where they win a goldfish I will never let them have.

We'd been to a different festival the week before in Boise. At that one, we'd seen a sign that stated: Frozen Key Lime Pie on a Stick Dipped in Chocolate. I was sold at Frozen Key Lime Pie on a Stick. Dipped in Chocolate really sealed the deal. But despite the fact that Mike and I agreed that this sounded awesome, we did not get one. We appreciated the idea of it but agreed that if we were going to consume excessive calories that day, which we were sure to do, it would most likely come in the form of beer.

After parking, my mother-in-law and I headed to the fair, towing the girls the rest of the way in a red wagon, and I decided that if there was Frozen Key Lime Pie on a Stick Dipped in Chocolate, I would buy one and make it my bitch. We had to park a few blocks away, because the event is a popular one, and people in the surrounding neighborhoods use the opportunity to set up lemonade stands, yard sales, and whatever else it is they want to offer up to the general public. In one yard sat a variety of pens that housed different animals. Nana, the girls, and I stopped to see what was there. Different pens held puppies, ferrets, and turtles for sale. Normally I would herd my clan away from this sort of display. We are strictly a no-pet household. In fact, I would be content if my houseplants died. As soon as I had a husband and two kids, I decided that I'd reached my limit of other living things to care for. It's not just that I'm cold, cruel, and heartless, only partially. The reality of why we are strictly a pet-free household is that we are in love with travel more than we are in love with pets. And the logistics of extended travel for a family of four is tough enough without needing to also arrange for the care of one's animals. But then I spotted a pen in the back that held my ultimate kryptonite: baby pigs.

I'd long held a fascination and adoration for baby pigs, and baby pot-bellied pigs in particular. Then, in one of my glorious former lives of cleaning houses, I'd cleaned a house where the family pet was a full-grown pot-bellied pig. Luna had a dog bed piled with blankets, and she would use her snout to burrow under the blankets and snuggle down until she was completely covered. From under there, she'd snuffle quietly until I began vacuuming, at which point Luna would emerge and snuggle up to her master in fear. After I'd finish vacuuming, Luna's owner would give me a small amount of shredded cheddar cheese to feed to Luna, because she knew that I was in love with her pig.

And now, heading to the Hyde Park Street Fair, we stopped outside a pen of four baby pot-bellied pigs. A woman in charge said, "Any of you are more than welcome to get into the pen and hold them or pet them."

"Amanda?" Nana said, well aware of my love for these odd little animals.

"No," I said wistfully. "I'd better not. I'll just admire from afar."

"That one over there." Nana pointed to the corner. "You can hardly even tell that one is a pig."

"Nana," I said, "that's a rabbit."

In the corner of the pen, apparently unperturbed by her swine roommates, sat a fluffy little bunny, roughly the same size as the baby pigs.

"Shit," Nana muttered, squinting at what she had thought was an unusually fluffy piglet.

The girls got back in the wagon, and we continued.

"Mama," Emilia said, "why can't we have a dog or a cat or a pig?"

"You know why we can't have any pets," I said. "We've talked about this before. If we had pets, we wouldn't be able to travel as much as we do. We wouldn't be able to go to Mexico and visit Nana and Papa."

"Mom," Ivy whined, "when are we going to go back to Mexico?" She sounded exasperated. "It's taking a long time."

"I don't know, sweetie. Every time we get on a plane, it costs a lot of money."

"Mom," Emilia said, "what about when Nana and Papa die?" Nana's eyes grew wide and startled. "Then can we get a cat?"

"Sorry, Nana," I said. "She really wants a cat."

I'm a big proponent of making kids walk at these types of events and leaving the wagon at home. But I actually wanted to look at some of the booths and see what the fair had to offer, and I knew such a thing would never happen unless the kids were occupied and carted around for at least a portion of the day. Otherwise they'd wear me down with complaints that their feet hurt until we'd either leave prematurely, just to escape the whining, or I'd end up carting someone around on my back.

We went first to the children's area, where I bought tickets that allowed them to go down a large, inflatable slide and play games at which Ivy won a goldfish that I did not let her have. We watched dancers perform folk dances from various cultures around the world, wearing traditional folk dress. After an hour of catering to the kids, we retrieved the wagon from where we'd parked it, bought cotton candy for the girls, and towed them as they stuffed their faces with spun sugar so that Nana and I could enjoy a beer and check out the booths. We passed by what appeared to be a discarded, bright blue condom on the ground, but I told myself that surely it was a popped balloon.

The cotton candy, sadly, did not buy us as much time as I'd hoped it would. When it was gone, we made our way over to the food trucks to survey the various fried offerings. I bought Emilia a giant pretzel, Ivy a giant corn dog, and they shared a giant lemonade. They ate in the wagon while Nana and I split a plate from the Hawaiian barbeque truck, not because it was what I craved the most, but because it was the only food truck with no line. My determination to eat whatever I wanted waned in the face of a twenty-minute wait for fried shrimp and onion rings. Young children are cold and callous when it comes to patiently waiting for a parent to finish her meal. I knew I had to order and eat before Ivy could down her giant corn dog.

Sadly, no one at the fair was selling Frozen Key Lime Pie on a Stick Dipped in Chocolate, and only after ordering the Hawaiian plate did I spot the giant turkey legs. I've never had a giant turkey leg, and it's on my bucket list. I will never order pulled pork or finger steaks because I find the combination of those words objectionable, but somehow I have no problem with the idea of walking around with a giant turkey leg clutched in my hand and gnawing on it like a caveman.

As Nana and I sat on the curb stuffing our faces, and Emilia and Ivy sat in the wagon stuffing their faces, a man with a dog on a leash struck up a conversation with the people seated next to us. The man was completely oblivious to us, but his dog was entirely focused on Ivy's corn dog. Ivy, meanwhile, began to tremble in terror as the dog leaned ever closer. I could sense that we were a second away from chaos and wailing. Three things happened at once. I scooped Ivy up and out of the wagon, Nana hollered at the man to watch his dog, and the dog's jaws snapped at the corn dog but caught only the open air left in the space where it had been. The man wasn't angry or malicious, just momentarily oblivious while in close proximity to a child who is afraid of dogs.

Sometimes when I tell people that Ivy is afraid of dogs, which is a polite way of saying, *Please control your dog and keep it away from my child,* they respond with, "Oh, but he's a nice dog." They don't understand that the temperament of their animal has absolutely nothing to do with the situation. It's sort of like asking someone with a fear of flying to board a plane, with the assurance that "This one is a really safe plane." Others have implied that we've fostered this fear in our daughter, despite the fact that we are not afraid of dogs and have managed to get Ivy to a place where she is completely comfortable with Nana and Papa's dog, Sitka.

After relocating the wagon to the other side, away from the man and his really nice, corn-dog-loving dog, the girls were in full view of two policemen standing outside their cruiser, there to ensure that nobody got too rowdy at the Hyde Park Street Fair. A young boy walked up to the cops, and they showed him the inside of their police cruiser. Within three minutes, the cops were swarmed by a herd of twelve other children, including Emilia and Ivy.

"Hi, kids! Come on over!" one of the policemen said. "You want to take a look?"

"That's where you put the bad guys," Emilia stated, pointing to the backseat and its caging.

"Would you like a sticker?" He handed out Junior Officer stickers to all of the kids, and most of them dispersed after that.

"Emilia," I whispered. "Ask him what's on his belt."

"What are all these things for?" Emilia walked up to him, and for a moment I thought she was either going to grab his gun or his crotch.

He took a step back and said, "These are all the things I need, just like Batman."

Emilia and Ivy looked unimpressed.

"My kids have never seen *Batman*," I explained with a hint of apology.

"Oh, well…" He started to explain what the various objects on his belt were but then trailed off as Emilia and Ivy turned their backs to him and walked away. "Seriously?" He held up his hands.

I tried to stifle my laughter and mumbled an apology to him for my girls' behavior. Apparently, they are not the least bit impressed by a man in uniform.

After lunch, we made another quick pass through the booths before heading to the playground for a while before heading home. They giggled, ran, screamed, and cried throughout the massive jungle gyms. Nana and I sat on a park bench and watched. From my peripheral vision, I saw something fly over my head. I looked to where the object had come from and identified the source as a small pack of teen-aged boys. I turned to look where the object had landed and saw that it was an unwrapped condom in vibrant red. I looked back at the boys and saw other condoms, still in their wrappers, littering the ground.

I stood up and bellowed, "Really? Pick it up. Pick them all up *right now!*" The boys giggled but scurried to retrieve them all. I didn't want them to giggle. I wanted them to feel the full impact of my fury. "You're throwing condoms at the Hyde Park Street Fair? You are throwing condoms at the *playground?* You are *pathetic!* Are your parents here?" None of them answered, and they ran away, which was certainly in their best interests.

I'm all for Planned Parenthood and for educating the public about birth control and the importance of preventing the spread of sexually transmitted diseases, but this isn't the first time that their presence at an outdoor festival has led to condoms littering the ground, used as playthings by immature boys. Perhaps the person manning the Planned Parenthood booth should scrutinize the people taking their condoms a little harder. Or come right out and say, "Really? Do you really think you're going to get laid? Because I'm going to guess you have a good four years to go, and by that time, these condoms will be past their expiration dates. So why don't you come see us in another few years." Okay, I know that would innately contradict the point of it all, but still, that's the sort of tactic we need to implement to separate the men from the boys. To keep the playground from being littered with rubbers. This seems to me like a terrible waste of perfectly good condoms. Maybe I should have hollered at them, "There are plenty of less fortunate people who don't have Planned Parenthood at their local street fair, there are horny people in Africa that don't have condoms, and here you are wasting some!" I hope at the very least that their parents found condoms later and that this led to uncomfortable conversations about the importance of condoms and the appropriate place in which to use them. And I hope those boys listened, because I don't want them reproducing.

***

CHAPTER SEVEN

Dear Disney, What the Fuck?

The behavior of teenage boys can be frightening, but it's more so when you are the mother of girls. Having to deal with teenage girls is going to be hard enough without the lingering presence of teenage boys. I'm not completely prejudiced against them, and I've met some well-mannered ones, but there are others out there. Boys who do awful, nasty things like hock loogies and kick puppies when no one is looking. And I'm especially terrified when I think about how obsessed Emilia is with one day getting married and having a baby. She complains all the time that it's going to take so long until she can have a baby of her own.

"Yes, it is going to take a long time," I told her. "You have to wait until you are at least twenty-five." This is the same age that I've told her she has to be before she gets any tattoos.

"But Mommy waited until she was *thirty*," Mike hastily added. I waited until I was thirty to have a baby, but I'd long since been tatted.

"Yes, I sure did."

"But that's going to take *forever*," Emilia whined. "I want to have a baby now."

"Well, pretty soon we'll have two new babies in the neighborhood to play with." We had two neighbors with babies on the way.

"Can I watch when their babies come out?" Emilia asked.

"No, that's not going to happen. But don't worry, if school is anything like it was when I was growing up, you'll see a video in health class in a few years and then hopefully change your mind about wanting a baby so soon."

She ignored the health class remark. "How do babies get out of their mommies' tummies?"

"Well, there are two different ways that can happen," I said. I then managed a clumsy but truthful explanation of a vaginal birth, couched in terms like "hole down by your pee pee."

"What's the second way?" she asked.

"The second way," I pulled up my shirt and pushed down the top of my jeans, "is they cut you open right here. See my scar? And they take the baby out that way."

"They cut you?" she gasped.

"Yes," I confirmed.

"Did you die?" Ivy asked.

"Nope, I didn't die."

"Did you bleed?" Emilia squirmed.

"Yes."

"How did they close your cut?" Ivy asked. For a split second, I'd thought she'd said a four-letter c-word.

"They just sewed me back together."

"So how come you did it that way?" Emilia asked, pointing at my C-section scar.

"Because your sister," I glared at Ivy, "refused to assume the correct position."

"I'm not ever having a baby," Ivy asserted.

With Ivy, we have less to worry about in terms of both marriage and babies, at least at this exact moment in time.

"And I don't want to get married," Ivy said.

"You don't have to," I responded.

"And since you're four years old, you don't have to worry about that just yet," Mike said.

"But I'm six," Emilia stated, as if this made it clear that the issue was more pressing in her case.

"I don't want to marry a boy," Ivy clarified.

"Well, you can marry a girl if you want," I said. "Or you don't have to get married at all. And Daddy's right, you don't have to decide right now."

"Actually, I can't get married," Ivy said.

"Because you're only four?" Emilia asked.

"No, I can't get married because I don't know how to dance with a boy. Or a girl."

"Don't worry," I assured her, "you have plenty of time to learn how to dance."

"But still," Mike interrupted, "that doesn't mean you have to get married if you don't want to."

"Mom, can we see your wedding dress?" Emilia asked.

"Yeah, Mommy. We want to see your wedding dress," Ivy echoed.

"You do?"

"Yeah! Yeah!"

"Okay," I agreed. I'd shown it to them before. It's not a traditional wedding dress, just a simple white dress that my mother bought me from the mall. I've worn it on a handful of occasions since the wedding; it was a good buy. It's also a good way to keep me from getting too fat. Every few years, when the right event presents itself, I unearth the dress. If I can't fit into it, I've strayed too far from my twenty-two-year-old body and resolve to make my fat ass less fat.

The girls followed me down the hallway and into their room, where my closet is. We live in a home that was built in the late fifties, when people had dressers and wardrobes instead of closets the size of my living room. Space is a premium, and as a result, my closet is in my daughters' bedroom. It's not a huge deal having a closet in another room. Until you have houseguests staying with you, and you at one point find yourself naked in your bedroom, and you have to figure out a way to get to the closet across the hall. Mike uses the closet in our bedroom, so of course I always have the option of putting on some of his clothes until I retrieve my own. Maybe it's the thrill-seeker in me, that tiny part of me that throws caution to the wind, flying in the face of the more dominant side of me that follows all the rules and does things the right way. But most of the time, instead of donning my husband's clothes, I open my door just a crack, peer down the hallway, and when I feel the time is right, do a giant naked leap across the hall and into the girls' bedroom, where I can retrieve my own clothes.

Emilia and Ivy trotted behind as I walked to their room and opened my closet. I pulled the garment bag out and fumbled with the zipper.

"Is that your wedding dress?" Emilia asked, giggling and referring not to the dress, but to the garment bag.

"Is that it, Mommy?" Ivy chanted.

"No, this is not my wedding dress," I protested. I had an image of myself walking down the aisle in a large garment bag, and somehow this slightly offended me.

The girls made up for it by oohing and ahhing as I unzipped the garment bag and gave them a peek at the dress, promising that they could wear it at their weddings someday if they wanted. Chances are that if they get married, neither of them will be content with a hand-me-down dress, which is not actually a wedding dress, originally purchased for two hundred dollars at a shopping mall, and will instead insist on a monstrosity of fabric and beads costing thousands of dollars, but one can cling to hope.

"When I get married, I'm going to live in a castle," Emilia stated.

"Not me," said Ivy. "I want to live in a hotel. And it'll have a giant swimming pool."

On the handful of occasions when we've stayed in a hotel, the girls are usually thrilled. Who am I kidding, I'm thrilled too. Though not for the same reasons. While the girls like the opportunity to sleep in the same big bed, jump on the big bed, and catapult themselves off of the big bed, I'm more enthralled with surroundings that I do not have to clean. There are no dishes to be done. It's a little bit of heaven. At least, most of the time.

When we all flew to California to celebrate Mike's grandfather's ninetieth birthday, Nana inexplicably booked all the family members into what is quite possibly the shittiest hotel in California. And it wasn't as if she'd booked the hotel without knowing the full extent of its shittiness. On the contrary, she'd actually stayed there before. Maybe she found the film of grime endearing. Maybe she thought sleeping in sheets that were surely to contain a wealth of other living organisms exciting. It wasn't overly cheap, so I can't attribute her continued patronage of the establishment to financial prudence. There was just something about the crumbling structure that appealed to her. Perhaps one day I'll find out that she has a secret life as a crack dealer and that she multitasked during this particular trip, combining the family celebration with a little drug dealing on the side. Whatever the case, it might have been the grossest hotel I've ever stayed in. And that's saying something. As soon as we opened the door to our room, I was knocked over by the smell.

"Oh my god," Mike said.

"Do they rent this place by the hour?" I wondered aloud.

"Awesome!" the girls squealed, running into the room. Maybe a full sense of smell doesn't develop until puberty. Or perhaps my kids find rank odors to be charming. In any case, they were oblivious to the stench and immediately flung themselves down onto the stained, worn carpet.

"Ooh, carpet!" Emilia said.

"It's so soft," Ivy cooed.

The carpet was not soft. The carpet was matted and gross and probably home to all manner of cooties.

"Girls," Mike barked. "Get up off the floor. Don't touch anything."

"Sorry, Daddy," they said in unison as they stood. Then they held hands and gleefully jumped on the bed, where they took turns smothering each other in what I can only assume was meant to serve as a bedspread.

"Dear lord," I gasped. "I think I'd rather they lick the carpet."

"Off the bed, girls," Mike boomed. "Just try and stand there and don't... move."

"We're just dropping our stuff off," I added. "Then we're going down to the pool."

"I thought you said the pool was too cold," Emilia questioned.

"It is," I admitted. "But even I will take a freezing pool over this room."

"But we love it here," Ivy whined. "We want to stay here and play."

Our home in Boise has hardwood floors. They are, well, hard. And usually cold. As a result, my children suffer from an acute case of carpet envy. Whenever they are in a place with carpet, even hard, worn, crappy, contaminated carpet, they throw their bodies on the floor and begin rolling around like cats in catnip.

Mike often takes the girls along with him when he shows houses to clients. They've been known to writhe around on a carpeted floor, and I fear that Mike's clients will get the impression that when home, we keep them locked up in a basement, chained to a cold concrete floor.

During the trip to California, and to Emilia and Ivy's dismay, we spent as much time as we could outside of the hotel room. This resulted in hours sitting by the pool, though it was too cold to do so. We opted to freeze instead of choke on the smell of the room. Much like their underdeveloped sense of smell, my girls also have that unique quality of small children to be impervious to freezing pool water. Between the stinky room and the freezing pool, they were in heaven, and the entire experience solidified their love of hotels.

"I changed my mind," Emilia said thoughtfully. "When I get married, I want to live in a hotel, too."

Emilia's obsession with marriage and both of the girls' obsessions with princesses comes largely from Disney. In the Disney movies, a happy ending doesn't refer to a hand job in a strip-mall massage parlor, but instead means the prince and princess get married. In *The Little Mermaid*, Ariel marries Prince Eric in the end, in a wedding dress with enormous shoulders. Tiana marries Prince Naveen at the end of *The Princess and the Frog*, and *Sleeping Beauty* concludes with Princess Aurora wedding Prince Philip after that bitch of a witch is vanquished. Cinderella marries her prince, and one assumes that Snow White's prince marries her instead of just riding away on his horse with her in order to get busy somewhere that's out of sight of the dwarves. The idea of doing the nasty in front of other people is creepy to me, but the idea of being spied on by seven dwarves is downright terrifying.

The over-employed Disney princess ending is so common that it's no wonder Emilia is in love with dresses and things that sparkle and wants some day to marry a prince. Perhaps we need to watch more *Pocahontas*, where it just doesn't work out in the end because, well, sometimes it just doesn't work out. But I have another problem with *Pocahontas*, or more specifically, with her would-be suitor John Smith. He and Pocahontas are the characters that try to bring about peace and understanding and acceptance of a culture that's different from their own. But I have a hard time believing in John Smith, since he's voiced by Mel Gibson, who seems so conflicted and depressed and desperate, on so many different levels, that I can't imagine him bringing about any sort of peace.

I love the movie *Brave.* I love it so much that not only did I spring for the expensive movie theater when it first came out, I actually went twice. And Ivy loves the movie *Brave.* Once she came to terms with her fear of the bad bear, she embraced it wholeheartedly. Honestly, I had to do the same thing. That is one scary bear. But how can you not love the tale of a feisty Scottish princess bucking the system that would force her to marry? All with a longbow in hand and the coolest animated hair ever to grace a movie screen? And unlike Mel Gibson, I adore Emma Thompson and really think that if she just got to know me, we'd be great friends. I've loved her in everything, from *Henry V* to *Men in Black 3.* And I cry at the end of *Brave* every single time I see it, even though I've seen it forty-seven times. But whenever I suggest we watch it, Emilia protests. For the longest time, I could not pinpoint her aversion to this movie. Is it the big scary bear? Is she frightened of the Scottish Highlands? Does the mother-daughter theme make her uncomfortable because, really, she wishes that Emma Thompson was her mother and not me? Could I really blame her if that was the case? How could she not love this movie? Merida is, after all, a princess. But Merida doesn't want to get married, won't be forced into it, and doesn't wear things that are pink and sparkly, and I think that because she doesn't marry a prince in the end (sorry for the spoiler), it ranks low on Emilia's list of favorites. She wants the damsel to be in distress, to be saved by the prince, and for the two to ride off into the sunset.

When it comes to kids' movies, I'm no expert. Wait. You know what? Screw that. I *am* an expert. I've seen them all, many, *many* times. To keep this knowledge current, I took my daughters to see *Frozen*. We joined aunts, cousins, nieces, and nephews to stuff our faces with expensive junk food and allow ourselves an hour and a half of escapism and entertainment. *Frozen* was great. It had everything you'd hope for in this type of movie. Music, comedy, a bit of danger, but not so much that your four-year-old will suffer subsequent nightmares. The movie had princesses in it, but just as in *Brave*, the princesses have a touch of bad-ass in them and don't require a prince to waltz in and save the day.

Later that evening, we joined other family members, and they asked how the movie was. We all agreed that we'd thoroughly enjoyed it. The kids volunteered their favorite parts of the movie: "I liked the little snowman." "I liked the reindeer." "I liked it when the princesses sang." "My favorite part was that I got to drink soda."

Then one of the adults chimed in about something I'd noticed. Something I'd been uncomfortable with but hadn't given voice to. She said, "The only thing that bothered me was when the queen is suddenly moving her hips all sexy."

I knew the exact moment she referred to. The queen sang a song and suddenly walked with an added hip move. It drew the eyes to the crotch. Her hips flared out with each step, and the animators even went so far as to show an indentation of the dress, just so you knew exactly where her groin was. She went from animated queen to animated real housewife of Disneyland.

The queen is skinny and beautiful. That was to be expected, and I accept the fact that I constantly have to instill in my girls a greater emphasis on kindness than body size. I accept that I must continually combat the impression they get from all of the skinny and beautiful princesses Disney creates and all of the skinny and beautiful people whom the rest of the media seems to worship, even when those beauties display horrific behavior. But the stripper hip shake was unnecessary.

After seeing the movie, I ranted online about it, and one of my friends told me I was overreacting. Maybe he's right, and I've simply grown too uptight. Maybe it's perfectly natural that while the queen croons her messages about independence and testing limits and breaking free from pretending to be something you're not for the sake of others, she accompanies these messages with body language that says, "Hey, everybody, look at my crotch!" Whether it's my overbearing nature or not, I'm still unsettled by showing these images to my daughters, and I freely acknowledge that my discomfort may have something to do with their early and unnatural gravitation to skanky hotel rooms.

* * *

CHAPTER EIGHT

The Traveler

Our neighborhood association, which is kind of like a homeowners' association, but you don't have fees, they don't tell you what to do, and they are not assholes, puts on an annual Family Movie Night in the park. It's free to attend, and everyone brings chairs and blankets and snacks, spreading out on a huge lawn adjacent to our neighborhood playground, in front of a giant inflatable screen. The movie they were showing was *Wreck-It Ralph,* and I thought it would be fun for us all to go watch it together. I offered to take two of the neighbor kids with us, an older girl and boy. I like doing this because it makes me seem like a really wonderful neighbor randomly offering free child care. In reality, I do it because my own children are easier to manage and happier if they have friends along.

We loaded up the wagon with blankets and snacks, rallied all of the children, and Mike, Nana, and I herded them down to the park. I took my travel coffee mug, which travels just as well with red wine as it does with coffee. The screen was enormous, and we staked out our spot to watch the movie. There was plenty of room for everyone to spread out. As I unpacked our snacks and got the kids situated, the neighbor girl who'd joined us announced, "I didn't eat dinner."

It was eight-thirty at night, and the rest of us had eaten dinner, so our snacks were fairly meager. In addition, they all seemed to contain ingredients to which the neighbor was allergic. "Okay," I said, "then I guess you and I better head back to your house to get you some food before the movie starts."

"Okay," she agreed. "That's a good idea."

We walked up the hill to her house, where she gathered food that wouldn't result in the need for an EpiPen, and then went back to the park. With the kids finally situated and the movie about to start, we settled in.

Five minutes into the movie, which I might add is a movie Mike enjoys, he leaned over to me and said, "Yeah, I'm not really into this. Not sure how long I'm going to last."

"What?" I said. "You're going to leave us?"

He squirmed, but only slightly, before saying, "Yeah."

"Lame."

"Yep, still leaving." This was one of those instances when Mike wasn't keen on the idea from the beginning, but he silently went along with it because he knew I was excited about it. Until the time actually came, at which point he bailed.

"Okay, but keep your phone on you. I'm calling you when the movie is almost over so you can come back and help us get all this stuff and all these kids home."

"Okay."

Although I had wanted it to be a family affair, I had my wine and my kids, so not all was lost. Then Ivy spotted a girl from her preschool and went to sit with her. The neighbor boy found friends of his own, and Emilia and the neighbor girl went to sit by themselves right in front of the screen. I looked at Nana. She shrugged and held her own not-actually-coffee-in-the-coffee-cup beverage up to mine, and we clinked.

"I guess it's just you and me," she said.

"I guess so."

About halfway through the movie, Ivy's friend left, and she returned to us. I abandoned my chair to sit with her on the blanket. Another family sat not far from us to our left. A man, a woman, a teenage boy, and two tween boys were there. All were watching the movie, except for the two tween boys, who each held a video game of some sort and chatted loudly back and forth. The rest of their family seemed adept at tuning them out. Aside from their chatter, I was constantly distracted by the glowing screens of their video games in my peripheral vision. I gritted my teeth, finished my wine, and wished I'd stashed a full box of wine in the wagon so that I could go for a refill.

The boys behaved much like Emilia did on the occasion when we let her play with an iPad, which is why we no longer let her play with an iPad. They were loud, obnoxious, engrossed, and oblivious to everyone and everything around them. I get the attraction of screens, I really do, but they were sitting with their video games in front of a fifty-foot inflatable screen. How is it that that is not enough entertainment for them, that they have to have their video games too? And why did their parents even bring them? Why not leave them at home, because clearly they were in such a state of love with their handheld devices that their surroundings were of no consequence.

In case you haven't seen *Wreck-It Ralph,* it takes place in the world of video games, with scenes ranging in scope from old-school, Pac-Man-like games, to Candyland-esque settings, to first-person shooter games. Until now, I never actually believed that I would have cause to use the phrase first-person shooter. I thought the boys would perhaps retire their video games and watch the movie when the first-person shooter scenes came on. These have been tempered from what real first-person shooter games must be like, enough to accommodate a much younger audience. There's no slapping of hookers like in Grand Theft Auto or horrific scenes of war and gore, but still there are big guys with guns, and I thought the boys would tune in. But no such luck.

When the father took his shoes off and stretched out along the grass, letting his gnarly feet come to rest on the edge of my blanket, I reached my boiling point. "That's it," I said to Ivy. "Stand up." I could tell she was confused and momentarily wondered if she was in trouble, but she did as I asked. "We have to move because these people are so rude," I announced. Ivy stood there as I pulled our blanket ten feet away from them, and we snuggled in again. This left poor Nana now sitting entirely alone in a camp chair where we started, but I was so disgusted with the offending family that it was all I could do just to get away from them.

The level of my voice when I said that the family was rude was my indecisive level. When I want to be loud enough so that you hear me and fully experience my anger and disgust, but I also want to be quiet enough so that you don't hear me, because really, I'm a huge pansy with a fear of confrontation. So I find a volume that's somewhere in between the two.

It's my way of playing Russian roulette, leaving it to chance whether or not my annoyance goes unnoticed or erupts into a full brawl at Family Movie Night in the park. If I ever make the news, it will probably be because of some stupid situation like that. *Uptight Woman Causes Chaos Over Innocent Pair of Feet.*

I made the news the last time we were in the park for a neighborhood event. It was for National Night Out, and I'd heard that neighborhood families were invited to attend and bring picnics, and that a fire truck would be there for the children to tour. I'm a sucker for a picnic, and Emilia is a sucker for a handsome fireman, so I really wanted all of us to go.

We had our picnic, and the girls got hats and stickers and temporary tattoos from the firemen. All of the firemen present had porn mustaches, and Emilia looked slightly disappointed that they were not as handsome as a fireman she'd fallen in love with once on a fieldtrip. Perhaps she gets this reaction from me. I'm not anti-mustache by any means, but sometimes I find myself confronted with a mustache that for some reason makes it impossible for me to take the owner of the mustache seriously. If I was in an emergency situation and one of these firemen came to my aid, I think I'd probably die, because I wouldn't be able to follow any of the life-saving instructions he'd be giving me. Instead, I'd just be staring at the porn mustache and trying to figure out what he wanted to communicate with the 'stache as I lay bleeding to death or inhaling oodles of deadly smoke. In this manner, I regard mustaches as a public health hazard.

Sandi's husband, Matt, occasionally cultivates this type of ridiculous facial growth. That's fine, completely his choice, but it does hinder his efforts to train all family members to refer to him as Handsome Uncle Matt. Similarly, my husband's addiction to *MacGyver* reruns and affinity for singing Michael Jackson songs while working out are not helping his efforts to get the family to call him Cool Uncle Mike.

While at National Night Out, we saw a display from the police K-9 unit, during which one officer commanded the dog to attack a man in a big padded outfit designed for just such occasions. It later occurred to me that this may not have been the best way to combat Ivy's ongoing fear of dogs. After the demonstration, the officer took questions from the crowd.

An older lady in a visor raised her hand. "Can't you get some sort of bulletproof vest for the dog? I mean, in a dangerous situation, how are you going to keep the dog safe?"

I tried to picture the dog clad in Kevlar. Wouldn't that impede his speed and stealth? And weren't speed and stealth his important additions to the force?

"Well, ma'am," the officer cleared his throat, "it's actually the dog's job to keep us safe. That's what he's there for."

"Yeah," she said. "But what if the dog gets injured? I mean, he could run the risk of getting shot or something."

The officer seemed to be trying his best to gently explain to the woman that as awful as that would be, a scenario in which the dog gets shot is preferable to a scenario in which an officer gets shot. She didn't look like she necessarily agreed.

"But I'd just hate to think that the dog could get hurt somehow," she continued. It was evident that she had no such reservations about the human police officers getting hurt.

"Ma'am, I don't know what else to tell you." The officer, who no doubt had dealt with all manner of criminal in his career, looked like he was at a loss on how to deal with the little old lady in the visor.

"Because, you know, the dog could die!" She said this as if the possibility hadn't yet occurred to anyone else. And she was silent for a moment, waiting for a reaction from the rest of the crowd, waiting for us all to see her point, because in her mind, we surely hadn't considered this possible outcome for the animal.

"Ma'am," the officer's voice was a little sharper now, "I'm going to be completely honest with you. The best possible thing for this dog would be to die doing his job." The woman gasped. "This dog loves his job. And there's going to come a time when he can't work anymore, and I would hate to see him have to retire. He'd be miserable. So if he's working and does a great job, and he were to get shot in the process and die, well then that would be okay."

"Is the dog going to die, Mama?" Emilia looked at me fearfully.

"No, honey," I assured her.

"But why does the man want to shoot the dog?" Ivy whispered.

"I promise, no one's going to shoot the dog."

"Maybe we should move away from this conversation," Mike muttered. "Let's head home."

"Okay," I agreed.

As we started to pack up our things, a man with a camera approached us.

"I'm from Channel Six," he said. "Mind if I ask you a few questions?"

"Sure," I answered. "Why don't you ask *them.*" I motioned to Mike and Emilia, but Mike just smiled and pulled the girls in front of him for a hug, thereby deflecting the cameraman back to me. I'm vain and love an audience, but my hair was in a bun, I had no makeup on, and I really did not want to be on camera. What if he zoomed in and saw my grotesquely large pores? Suddenly my nose itched, and I feared that something was hanging out of it. We'd had veggies and hummus during our picnic, so I probably had broccoli stuck in my teeth. The red light of the camera went on.

"So, tell us what brought you down here tonight," he said.

"Oh, uh, well, we love a picnic," I said.

"And..."

"And we heard there was going to be a fire engine."

"And..."

"And it just seemed like a great opportunity to get to know some of the neighbors." *Perfect,* I thought. *He can't possibly need more than that.* But the cameraman didn't think so.

"But, can you talk a little bit about National Night Out and why this is important?" he asked.

It occurred to me then that this was more than just a neighborhood picnic. National Night Out was a National Thing. And it was apparently a National Thing that I didn't know about. There was a specific point or goal to it, and I was participating without even knowing what that was.

"Um, well yeah, I think it's really important..." I trailed off. Suddenly I had the terrifying thought that I was going to be seen on the news saying that a cause was really important, and maybe that would be a cause I don't actually support. What if my haggard face was being recorded supporting something really terrible? What if National Night Out was an event to drum up support for the KKK or pedophiles? What if I was supporting an organization for the oppression of gay people, or a political group that wanted to continue starting wars in other countries in the hope that America would eventually achieve world domination?

"Well, how concerned are you about the crime that's happened recently here?" he asked.

Aha! That's why we had police and firemen. It was about neighborhood crime prevention or something similar, not just picnicking in the park with your family. A vague recollection of the cause was coming back to me.

I muttered something about how it was really important to know your neighbors and of course I was concerned with the recent crime in the neighborhood. This was partially true. Our neighborhood had experienced its fair share of break-ins and petty theft, and these crimes had been on the rise in recent years, but it had been almost two years since the last murder on our street, so really I thought we were doing pretty well. I thought maybe the neighborhood should have a central sign with numbers posted on how many days it had been since the last break-in, car theft, murder, et cetera. Sort of like a factory posting how many safe days they've had since the last time someone's fingers got chewed up in a machine. It could really boost morale. Maybe I'd talk to the powers that be of this National Night Out organization about my great idea. It could become standardized in cities across Idaho. Wait, this was national. Across the nation! They'd probably ask me to be on their board of directors. Maybe even want to make me president.

"I love you, Mom. I love you, Mom. I love you, Mom." Ivy broke free of Mike and inserted herself in between me and the camera. It was very cute, except for the fact that she'd screwed up the last of my mumbling, and after Mike removed Ivy, the cameraman asked me to repeat my incoherent rambling, which I sensed was getting more incoherent the longer I spoke.

When we finally made our exit that evening, I was glad that when it aired on the ten o'clock news that night, I'd be fast asleep. Being on the news is great, until you see yourself on the news, and all of your feminist beliefs about being happy with your size and shape fly out the window, and you resolve not to eat for the next few days, because the person they said was you that spoke on the television looked like the sumo version of you. It looked like you after being distorted through some sort of computer app that's supposed to be funny but is really just disturbing. And the camera doesn't add ten pounds. That's a fucking pipe dream. The camera adds sixty-five pounds.

When *Wreck-It Ralph* ended during movie night, I scowled over at the other family, but they appeared to exist in a continual state of obliviousness, so I concluded that we wouldn't end up in a brawl, after all. Everyone was tired and cold, and Ivy appeared to be hovering just shy of a meltdown.

I gathered up the children, our blankets, and chairs, relieved to find that no one and nothing had been lost during the evening. Even Mike had returned, of his own accord and without me having to call for help, to assist in getting everyone back home.

"What did you do at home?" I asked.

"A little bit of work. Watched a little of the game."

Aha. It hadn't occurred to me that there might be a football game on. I'm lucky in that my husband likes sports a little, but he's not obsessed like many men. He doesn't wear jerseys on game day or hang out at sports bars or insist on having a farting pack of men invade our living room for an afternoon. But every now and then, he likes to watch a little football. Normally I don't begrudge him this, but I was still bitter that he'd abandoned movie night.

"Football," I said, as if uttering the name of another woman.

"How was the movie?" Mike asked as we walked back up the hill.

He knew how the movie was, because we'd both seen the movie a million times. We owned the movie. What he was really asking was how the experience was, because that's why I'd forced the event on all of us, because I wanted the experience. And Mike had left not just because of the football game, but because he knew somehow, long before I did, that the experience would not actually be what I wanted it to be. And sometimes, when our spouse really wants to do something that we know won't turn out well, we just have to let them find out for themselves.

"I don't want to talk about it," I said.

* * *

CHAPTER NINE

Added Protein

The first time I saw the first-person shooter scenes in *Wreck-It Ralph,* I was tempted to turn it off. Wasn't this supposed to be a kids' movie? I'd gone from watching the harmless and unintelligible Q-bert to seeing Jane Lynch made into a sexy, hard-ass soldier wielding high-tech, rapid-fire weapons. Sure, this was an alternative view of women when compared to all of the Disney princesses, but did we really have to have war and slaughter be a part of it? I realized that since I have only girls, I haven't been exposed to the same level of gun play as other parents. My world is glitter and stickers and sequins. We don't even allow our kids to have water guns. Not so much because of the gun factor, but because I can think of few things as annoying as having my child squirt water at me.

I'm not a gun person. I grew up not far from Baltimore and D.C., so I associated gun culture primarily with drive-by shootings. Guns were constantly in the news, and usually in regard to a story in which bad guys killed innocent people. It never occurred to me to associate guns with hunting animals for food.

Mike grew up hunting in Alaska and therefore has a very different impression of guns. Here in Idaho, the prevailing attitudes lean much further toward his upbringing than mine.

"Do you ever miss hunting and fishing with your dad?" I asked him.

"Ugh," he answered. "It's really hard work."

"I thought you just shoot something and eat it."

He looked at me with mild disgust and shock. "There's a lot more to it than that."

"Like what? Don't you just kill something and then put it on a metal bar thingy. And then you turn it slowly over a fire while someone heats beans in a tin cup and someone else plays the harmonica?"

"It's called a spit, not a metal bar thingy. And the image you're talking about is from westerns you saw as a kid. That's not even close to what hunting was for me growing up."

"So what's the difference?"

"Well, first of all, you're not out on the frontier hunting your dinner for that night. You're hunting a larger animal that you can use to feed your family all winter. So if you even get one, you then have to skin it and pack out the meat. You start cutting around the asshole, and you want to do so carefully. If you break open the bowels, you have a whole new mess on your hands."

"Wait, how did we get here?"

"Where?"

"To this conversation. Because of all the things about which I am certain in this world, highest on the list is that I do not want to hear the details about cutting around the asshole of a dead animal."

"Well, you asked."

"I just wondered what was so hard about it. Beyond dressing up in camouflage and spritzing yourself with deer piss."

"I have never spritzed myself with deer piss," Mike asserted.

"Are you sure?"

"Uh, yeah. I'm pretty damn sure. I think you must have gotten that idea from a movie or something."

"I don't know. I swear I remember you spritzing yourself with deer piss at some point."

"First of all, guys don't spritz, okay? And B, anytime I've spritzed, it's been with something to mask the human smell and the smell of laundry detergent and stuff like that."

"Fine," I conceded. "So what's the hard part?"

"In Alaska," he explained, "a lot of the time you have to hike miles and miles up mountains before you get to the place where you start hunting. You're cold, tired, and spend hours walking. Sometimes you don't even get anything. And if you do get something, you have to pack it out. It's exhausting."

"So it's just a lot of waiting around then?"

He looked at me with an intense and level stare. "I've never waited. I hunt."

When I asked him about the downsides of hunting, I thought he would talk about moral dilemmas regarding pulling the trigger, or a tearful moment as you stand over a dead doe and watch Bambi mournfully watching you from the shadows before he scampers off in search of a skunk to befriend in his grief. I thought the skinning and dismembering of an animal would rank somewhere in the list of Not Great Things About Hunting, but I was wrong.

"Then why do it?" I asked. My husband has never felt

the thrill of the kill, been enthusiastic about guns, or dared suggest we mount some sort of head on a wall.

"Because we could get an entire freezer full of meat," he said. "Up in Alaska, we couldn't really afford cow meat. Everything shipped up there was so expensive."

"Cow meat?"

"Yeah, you know, like steaks and hamburger."

"We call that beef. Nobody calls it cow meat."

"Whatever. A lot of people couldn't afford it. Most people hunted and fished. For meat, most of the time we had deer meat."

"I believe they call that venison."

Though Mike doesn't hunt anymore, my father-in-law still goes every year, often to different places with friends he's known for forty years. He hunts with a bow, which seems perhaps more barbaric than a rifle. But on the other hand, hunting with a bow is harder, because you have to get much closer to the animal. This gives the animal a better shot at surviving, so you know, six of one, half dozen of the other.

While Nana and Papa inhabited our basement for a portion of the summer, they busied themselves getting Papa ready for an upcoming elk hunt. He would travel with two other men, two horses, and a mule to southern Idaho where the three of them would hunt with bows and try to kill a large, tasty woodland creature.

"Let's try this," Nana said to Papa one morning in the kitchen as she made him a cup of coffee from an instant packet of Starbucks. This was the beginning of a week-long dilemma over what sort of coffee situation would be best for Papa to take on his hunt. He didn't like instant coffee unless he had his French Vanilla-flavored coffee creamer with him. If he took creamer with him, he might not be able to keep it cold enough during the duration of the nine-day hunt. Powdered creamer was looked upon as sacrilege. If he took regular coffee, he would need a filter or means by which to brew it. And if he went that route, should he take Irish cream along to spike it? The questions over this issue were endless. As a result, Nana ended up running errands to buy him different coffees and various means of preparing it, and I was shocked at the effort she put in to readying him for a trip she would not be on. Why he didn't solve the problem, which wasn't really a problem, himself is beyond me. And if you are roughing it in the woods and sleeping in a hammock for nine days, can't you just make do with whatever is easiest for that period of time? Apparently the answer is no.

While Nana hemmed and hawed over keeping her husband well-caffeinated during his upcoming trip, Papa walked into the living room where the girls were dressed up in their fanciest dresses, for no other reason than sometimes dressing up is fun. They stood posing for him, beaming, waiting for praise.

"Holy Carumba!" he exclaimed, with arms spread wide. "You girls look beautiful!"

Holy Carumba is of course the bastard offspring of Aye Carumba and Holy Cow, a new addition to the already large collection of incorrect words and phrases adopted by my in-laws.

The girls giggled and ran off in search of sparkly shoes. Papa addressed me then. "So, I'm going in for an MRI today." He'd been seeing a variety of doctors and had been through a slew of assessments to prepare for neck surgery he'd undergo in the coming winter, a surgery that would hopefully alleviate neck pain he'd been experiencing for years, which had recently increased in intensity. "And the last time I had an MRI, it was twenty years ago. You have to lie back for like an hour and not swallow. It's horrible."

"I don't think I could do that," I said. I've long suspected that I have overactive salivary glands and am always embarrassed when visiting the dentist, as a mere seven seconds of lying back with my mouth open is enough to start me choking on my own spit.

"Hopefully I'm remembering it wrong, or it's different now," he said, as if there was a chance that being told to lie still without swallowing for the purposes of an MRI might have been a fabricated memory. "But I want to get this MRI taken care of before the hunt."

"So, how can you go hunting and kayaking if you have this neck issue?" In addition to his upcoming hunting trip, my in-laws had a nine-day kayak trip in Mexico planned for the fall.

"It's not so much the pain," he explained. "I'm having the surgery done because I can no longer look up, and if I try to, my vision goes black. It's all related to a problem in my neck."

"Yeah," I agreed, "that sounds like something you should probably get taken care of."

When Mike was growing up and would hunt with his brother and father, Nana would often accompany them and film parts of the hunt. Nana is undoubtedly much more of a bad-ass than I am, and I could not see myself ever being able to undertake such a task. I was raised not only with an entirely different view of guns and hunting, but also of meat in general. I was taught from early on to be squeamish with foods, to be suspect of anything less than sterile kitchen conditions, and to consider meat a little bit icky and entirely cruel. From the animals' perspective, you can't really debate the cruel part. But you know, circle of life and all that.

For about a decade spanning my mid-teens to mid-twenties, I was a vegetarian. This began in my teens for a few reasons, including that my sister was a vegetarian and she was cooler than me, so maybe I'd be cooler if I was more like her. What really put the vegetarian practice into action was working two summers on a farm in West Virginia. It wasn't just the brutality of farm life, but also the less than sterile kitchen conditions in which the meat was handled that turned me off entirely. So I spent most of my teens and the early part of my twenties as a vegetarian. After a decade without meat, steak suddenly and inexplicably sounded good, and I was over it. I've been an enthusiastic carnivore ever since.

When Mike and I first met, I was still a vegetarian, which was difficult for him to comprehend. His parents visited early on in our relationship and brought with them a pack of venison jerky from a recent hunt.

"Just try it," Mike said.

"I'm a vegetarian," I protested.

"You don't understand," Mike insisted. "This stuff is so good. My brother and I used to fight, physically, over this. We used to hide it from each other. It's like the best stuff ever."

"I don't eat meat," I stated. I wasn't sure how to make my position any more clear.

"Yeah, but just have a bite."

"Mike, I'm going to speak slowly. I do not consume the flesh of animals."

"Oh, come on. It's not like AA and you'll fall off the wagon with one bite."

As naïve and clueless as I was, and continue to be, in regards to hunting and the hunting culture, it holds a direct parallel to how naïve and clueless my husband was regarding what it is to be a vegetarian. In his mind, if someone told you something was tasty enough, or special enough, you should just have a bite anyway.

"It's a dead animal, Mike. Maybe that's fine for you, but some people think it's just gross."

"They're wrong."

"They're wrong?" I asked incredulously.

"Yeah. Gross is finding live worms inside a peach you've just bitten into. All tiny and white and wiggling around and wondering who turned the light on. And then you spit out what's in your mouth, wondering if you got any live ones in there, wondering if they're burrowing inside your body and laying little larvae. Biting into a peach with live worms in it, that's gross. At least with this," he held up the venison jerky, "I know it's dead."

He had a point. There have been a couple of instances over the years when trying to get my husband excited about a more vegetarian diet has backfired. The fresh peaches filled with worms were the beginning and made the idea of free, organic produce from a neighbor sound not as awesome as we'd previously thought. Then we were in a sushi joint, and I tried to get him on an edamame kick. Personally, I didn't really like edamame that much, but they were hugely popular, so I figured they'd grow on me. We gnawed our way through pod after pod, waiting to fall in love with the little green gems, until I split open a pod and found, freshly steamed, the same type of worm that had infested the free peaches, though this time lifeless. Now, when I watch others eating edamame, I can't help but wonder how many tiny, white worms they are consuming, without even knowing it. I've never been able to eat edamame since, except when it's whipped into hummus, and the little bugs are no doubt ground fine enough to where I don't really know they are in there.

We received a phone call during my father-in-law's nine-day hunt. The connection was not great, but he sounded exhausted and reported that they'd "taken down a monster elk."

I better get things ready, I thought. I started clearing out the freezer. How much elk meat came from a monster elk? Would it be packaged in individual bags of ground meat and steaks or would he want to string a bloody carcass up in our garage and bleed it out and butcher it there? And if so, would that prove to be a good learning experience for my girls? Would it toughen them up and introduce them to the realities of the world of meat or turn them into wussy little girls and give them nightmares about Papa the Butcher?

Be cool, I told myself. *Be cool. Remember, this sort of thing is normal to these people, so don't freak out.* By "these people" I meant my husband and my in-laws, but in the wake of the impeding elk or meat or carcass or however it should be referred to in whatever state it was in, "these people" seemed completely foreign, with alien ways and speaking in a language unfamiliar to me. They used the word *loin* way too often in relation to food, and what the hell was backstrap? I pictured a leather strap with which to beat on an animal's hide. Like a riding crop. And was that what tanning the hide meant? Would these things take place on our property?

I was just beginning to brace myself for the possibility that my garage would soon be turned into a scene from *Dexter,* and perhaps I should cover the floor with plastic sheeting, when my husband noticed my distress.

"They're not bringing back a big dead animal," he said.

"They're not?"

"No. By now they would have had to take it somewhere to have the meat processed."

"Oh, good."

"Believe me, I don't want an animal strung up in my garage, either. And if I ever hunt again and do get something, I'm paying a butcher to process the meat. I won't do it here."

"Oh, good," I said again. "But will you make me eat it?"

"Probably."

I cringed and took a deep breath, reminding myself how much I like a good steak. Especially since I don't have to see it until it's served to me. Denial of the origins of food is a powerful thing.

CHAPTER TEN

Crime Scene Kitchen

Papa's return from the hunt came late one night when his hunting companions dropped him off. We helped him unload his stuff, and one of the other men proudly showed me the rack. I know I was supposed to be impressed with the size of the antlers, but I couldn't get past the neatly sawed through crown of the skull to which the antlers were attached. Who gets the job of sawing off the top of the skull when the opportunity presents itself? Is it an honor, or is it better to be the one who first cuts around the asshole? Does one flip a coin?

It turned out that my father-in-law hadn't been the one to shoot the animal and therefore wasn't bringing back a freezer full of meat, after all. I know I was supposed to pat him on the back and offer words of encouragement like "Maybe next year, good try." But, really, I was ecstatic that I didn't have to sample various parts of an elk in the coming weeks. Instead he took only a few packages of ground meat and one package of steaks, also known as the backstrap. The man who'd gotten the elk, while hunting on his own away from the rest of the group, ended up paying a lot of money to process the meat, and therefore my father-in-law took only a little bit, what he felt was his fair share in exchange for helping to process the animal.

I love the term process. It's such a sterile word, so far removed from phrases like "cut around the asshole." I think of getting my kids ready for school in the morning as a process. I think of installing an appliance as a process. But as soon as you take that noun and make it a verb, it takes on a sinister tone, and I think of knives and cattle chutes and that creepy air gun thing from *No Country for Old Men* that was intended for cattle but that Javier Bardem used to fire invisible bullets of air into the brains of his victims. As if his hair wasn't creepy enough.

Nana was visiting her father in Washington when Papa returned from his hunt. I was glad she wasn't here, because I knew that if she was, she would spend a full day scurrying around doing his laundry and unpacking everything for him. Her absence forced him to do his own laundry. And when you've been living in the woods for nine days, I think no one should have to deal with the resultant stench other than the person who created it.

Papa's return came with stories about being thrown off a horse, knocked over by a horse, and assaulted by his own hammock in the middle of the night when he tried to get up to go pee and ended up flipping over, trapping himself in a facedown position within the folds of unforgiving fabric.

"You were trapped?" I asked for clarification.

"Well, I was trying to get out of the hammock, and when I swung one leg out, I somehow turned over and rolled myself up inside of it. I was sort of pinned in there. I'd be damned if I was going to wake up John and ask for help," he said, embarrassed, "but it took me about thirty-five minutes to wriggle out of it."

I wonder what John, his hunting partner, would have done if he had woken him. Would he immediately have rushed to my father-in-law's aid, full of concern, worried that the hammock was cutting off blood flow and slowly strangling him? Or more likely, would he have searched in the dark for a camera and woken up their third companion to fully appreciate the situation before offering assistance?

"So, how did you get out?" I asked.

"Well, I had the one leg out, and I had one arm out. I knew there were ropes above me, and I just had to pull on the right one."

The mention of multiple ropes made me think that this wasn't what I typically picture as a hammock, not a gentle cocoon strung up between two palms on a lazy beach. This was a hunting hammock, whatever that may be. Something in a lovely camouflage pattern that a hunter could sleep in or use as a means of trapping wayward game. In the middle of the night, my father-in-law had managed to combine both uses.

I'd hoped he would prepare the elk meat from the hunting trip on a night when I happened to be occupied at book club, where the attendees snack on hummus and gluten-free crackers, but he was eager to share the bounty. I reminded myself that this was a very special thing to him and that I should be grateful and do my best not to appear squeamish and snobby.

When I came home in the late afternoon from a Sunday at the zoo with Emilia and Ivy, I could tell that Papa had been busy in the kitchen that day preparing the meat. The meal would be a celebration of Nana's return from Washington. There was blood spattered on the floor, dried blood on the countertops, drops of blood on a note Nana had left. I opened the fridge. Elk steaks and ground elk sat defrosting on paper plates, soaking through them, meat hanging over the edges. I lifted up a bag of baby carrots to find it sitting in blood. While it looked to me like a serial killer had brutally dispatched a victim in my kitchen, my father-in-law was completely unaware of any mess or cause for concern. Maybe he likes his carrots bloody? Or was it a new dish, like carrots tartare, and I was just not cultured enough to know about it? But more likely, he simply does not see the same things that I see. I cleaned up the blood and placed the meat into glass containers to stem the spread of further contamination, then spent the rest of the afternoon doing my best to stay out of the kitchen, not look at the kitchen, and pretend that nothing was taking place in the kitchen.

In situations like these, I've learned that if I don't watch how my in-laws prepare food, I will enjoy it. Because, really, my father-in-law is an excellent cook. We simply have different approaches on what is and is not okay in terms of food preparation. And to be fair, not only is his food good, but I've never known anyone to get sick from anything he's prepared, so perhaps I just need to relax. Then again, I'm the one cleaning up the crime scene.

Before dinner that evening, Papa watched football on the couch, which turned into more of a marathon nap. And while he was sleeping, I took his picture, because there's something awfully sweet about seeing a sixty-seven-year-old man curled up in the fetal position like a four-year-old tuckered out from a big day of playing, or in his case, smearing my kitchen with blood.

As usual, the food turned out to be excellent, and I did my best through the meal to take tiny bites and try to suppress the squeamish vegetarian within who'd seen pictures of my father-in-law and his hunting companions posing with the unfortunate animal.

Since my in-laws continue to make goo-goo eyes at each other after nearly fifty years of marriage, they designated the following night as date night and went out to a romantic dinner to celebrate being reunited. In their absence, I texted Virgil.

Me: Want to come for dinner tonight?

Virgil: Sure. All I eat is cereal and Piehole, so food would be great.

The Piehole is a downtown pizza joint and apparently one of Virgil's new hangouts.

"How's work going?" Mike asked his brother when he showed up, scruffy and reeking of cigarettes, but certainly not the scruffiest or smelliest that we'd ever seen him.

"It's great. I love it. I'm at a house just down the street, finishing up the tile job. I work all night, nobody bothers me. I have to work naked sometimes because I just sweat, I mean my body just sweats until I can't stand it, and the only thing I can do is go stand outside because I just need to feel that cool air on my wet, sweaty skin."

"Ew," I said.

"But it's awesome, there's no one there, I just have a few beers, get my work done. I don't drink on the job. I mean, I've never been caught. At least I was never caught back when I did that. I haven't drank on the job in a really long time. Actually, I never have. I don't drink at all when I'm there. And I usually stop at Albertson's and get a bag of those chocolate chip cookies. Not just the regular kind of chocolate chip cookies," he paused, letting us know he was about to say something really important, "but the chocolate chip cookies that also have the M&Ms in them. That's key. Oh my god, they're so sexy. And one day I was there, and you know, I always open it up and eat one before I check out, and I tried one, and it wasn't right because that day they used real butter. Or didn't use real butter. Whatever, anyway, I just raised hell. I will get people fired over that shit."

I looked to Mike, expecting to see him smirk or roll his eyes, but his face was one of complete seriousness. "I love chocolate chip cookies," he whispered.

"Wow," I said. "You guys are very passionate about your chocolate chip cookies."

"It was Mom's fault," Virgil said solemnly.

"Totally," Mike agreed. "She forgot about them every single time."

"Burning cookies should be against the law. It totally ruins the experience."

"And growing up, did we ever have bread that wasn't burned?"

"No," Virgil said sadly, and you would have thought the brothers were reliving the death of a beloved pet. "But work is awesome," he said, snapping his head up and reanimating himself. "I know where to find all the stuff you need. All these other guys are ridiculous, spending all this time and money at

Home Depot or Lowe's or Ace. I hang out at the secondhand, used-parts construction store because I'm a smart guy. Man, I wish I was shorter."

"You are so hard to follow," I said.

"Or taller."

"Why would you wish you were shorter?" I asked. "I hate to break it to you, but you're not that tall to begin with." Virgil is only slightly taller than me and barely reaches 5'6".

"Bigger dick," he said.

"What?"

"If I was shorter, I'd have a bigger dick." He said this matter-of-factly, as if it was common knowledge. As if he could sacrifice an inch or two of height, and by compressing his body, the extra cells would move down to his penis and settle there.

"That's ridiculous," I said. Mike had no comment, and I wondered if he secretly believed this to be true.

"Just like the midget in Basic Training," Virgil continued.

"I don't believe they allow midgets in the army," I countered.

"Of course, the guy was the flag carrier, running around carrying the flagpole, but all you'd see was the flag bouncing around in the air 'cause he was so tiny. Guy had a huge dick. That's why it would be so awesome to be a dwarf."

"What are you talking about, Uncle Virgil?" Emilia said as she walked into the kitchen to join the adults. She and Ivy had been engrossed in playing Kitties, which involves a lot of high-pitched meowing, and I wondered when she had stopped being a kitty and started tuning in to Uncle Virgil. "Were you talking about *Snow White?*" she asked hopefully.

"Yes, I was," he said with confidence. "Can you name all the dwarves in *Snow White?*"

"Yes," she said with equal confidence. "Happy, Grumpy, Sneezy, Dopey, Sleepy, Bashful, and Doc."

"Wow," said Virgil. "I was not expecting that."

"I'm going to go back to playing Kitties now," she announced.

"I think that's a great idea," Mike commented.

In an effort to steer the conversation away from dwarf penises, or any penises for that matter, I asked Virgil what we should make for the holidays this year. Virgil is an excellent cook, and he and I often team up for the holiday meals. Even the height of summer is not too early to begin discussing possible accompaniments to the Thanksgiving turkey.

"I think we should try making something in a pumpkin," I said.

"Like some sort of squash dish that you bake in the actual pumpkin?" he asked.

"Exactly."

"No pasta," Mike said, running his fingers along the countertop.

This demand was the result of a past holiday when Virgil and I made our own butternut squash-stuffed ravioli. We'd never made our own pasta before and thought we'd give it a try. The preparations went well, until Virgil began cutting the sheets of pasta into squares. He was almost finished when we suddenly realized that with each cut, he was gouging deep knife marks into the counter of the kitchen island. We panicked.

"Don't tell Mike," he said.

"What if we put a tablecloth over it?"

"A tablecloth over your kitchen island? That's not going to hide it. That's going to be all weird and draw attention to it. Maybe he won't notice."

"He won't," I said.

And he didn't. What he did notice is that I spent much of the evening hovering over the kitchen island and glancing nervously at the counter every few seconds. "What are you doing?" he'd finally asked.

"Virgil and I made pasta and he cut into the counter and now there are these big knife marks all over and they don't come out," I blurted in a rush.

"Nice poker face, Amanda." Virgil sighed.

"I can't help it. You know I'm a shitty liar!"

"You guys should be thanking me," Virgil said. "I just gave you a distressed countertop. For free. Want me to gouge the rest of the counters so it all matches?"

I'd like to say that it was worth it. That the meal was so fabulous that our collective taste buds experienced a unique culinary ecstasy. Sadly, the meal fell just short of that. The pasta was tough. Okay, it was inedible, and everyone at the table spent the meal trying to hack into the ravioli and gain sustenance from the meager pocket of filling inside.

"Don't worry," Virgil assured his brother. "We won't make pasta. I don't do carbs anyway." This seemed suspect, given that he'd admitted his diet of late consisted of pizza, cereal, and chocolate chip and M&M cookies.

We continued discussing the possibilities of preparing a dish that would be cooked inside a pumpkin, or perhaps inside small, individual pumpkins, because wouldn't that make for a killer presentation? In the middle of the conversation, I started to feel way too domestic, because Virgil and I were engaged in full-on Martha Stewart speak. We used words like wild rice and quinoa and gazpacho. And the only thing I have in common with Martha Stewart is that she went to prison, and I've always secretly wanted to go to prison. I just imagine myself getting so much reading and writing done, and doing lots of pushups so that when I came out, my arms would look really buff. I wouldn't have to cook or do laundry, unless that was my job of course. But I hoped I could instead work in the library or make license plates. I think I'd be really good at making license plates. I could make the heck out of those license plates. It seems like work that would require some attention to detail and precision. I could totally do that. Sign me up. But beyond this prison connection, I don't really want to have much to do with Martha Stewart. I will not shop at K-Mart, I do not watch *The Today Show,* and I can guarantee I will never have any wine leftover, so I won't be freezing it into pretty little cubes. Just the thought of using wine for any purpose other than drinking makes my skin itch.

* * *

CHAPTER ELEVEN

Idaho: Like New York, Only Different

In the wake of my fear that I was becoming too domestic and would soon start crocheting doilies or saving pictures from Pinterest about fun things to do with the cardboard tubes from toilet paper, I decided that it was time for Mike and me to plan our next big family adventure. After all, we'd been back from the Jersey Shore for a full two months, so obviously we were getting a little stir crazy. We wanted to broaden our scope of possibilities a bit. We'd rented our house out on more than one occasion, done one-month trips to a few different places, and a three-month trip to Mexico. We were ready for a bigger step, so we started talking about a two- or three-month trip to some place farther away. I wanted our children to hear different accents and experience different cultures.

We listed our house on HomeExchange.com, and it quickly became my newest addiction. I reached out to families in New Zealand, Australia, Iceland, Hungary, and all over the United Kingdom. The only places I ruled out were Mexico and the U.S., simply because of the been-there-done-that factor. *This will be perfect,* I thought. *We'll find a family like ours who wants to trade homes for a few months. Surely someone out there wants to come to the U.S.* And it's true, there are plenty of homes listed by families looking to do a home exchange in the U.S. Unfortunately, none of those families want to come to Idaho. New York and San Francisco were the most popular destinations, and time after time, my inquiries were met with "We're not interested at this time" responses. I tried to sell Boise in all its glory. I took the secrets that Idahoans prefer to keep quiet and plastered them about the world. Cool downtown! Ski lifts! Views! Arts & Culture! I marketed our home to golfers, skiers, and wine enthusiasts. I wrote about hot air balloon festivals, the intricate and extensive park system, and a landscape with something for everyone. Perhaps I was shooting too high. Maybe I should have targeted people who really like potatoes or Frozen Key Lime Pie on a Stick Dipped in Chocolate, or run with the headline: Just Like New York, Only Different. In any case, I was disappointed as week after week went by with no takers.

My in-laws loved to offer input as to where they thought we should venture in the world, not because they wanted to make sure we made the most of our travels, but because any time we go someplace exotic, they're sure to find a way to visit us while we are there.

"Any luck on the home exchange?" my mother-in-law frequently asked.

"Don't worry, we're trying," I said.

"Because we really would like you guys to go someplace cool."

It's not that my in-laws are trying to leach on to our adventures. We leach on to them all the time, moving into their guesthouse in Mexico for months at a time, often encouraging them to make improvements on the place that would happen to benefit our family. Visits from Mike's parents are also encouraged because in addition to being fun to hang out with, they provide free child care.

I queried a home in Finland and wondered if we went there, if we'd end up eating more elk-like meals. I'd spent a day in Helsinki in my youth, on my way to do an exchange program in Moscow. I remember one of the other students ordered a reindeer sandwich. Throughout lunch, *Rudolph the Red-Nosed Reindeer* ran on a loop in my head, and I pictured the innocent Rudolph from the 1964 Christmas special, his little cartoon body splayed out in the Finnish snow, bleeding cartoon blood.

I noticed that every time I sent an inquiry, I did so with unflappable optimism. With each home I read about, I was sure that the people would respond positively. So when I inquired about the home in Finland, I was sure we would go to Finland. When a home in Australia caught my eye, I was sure we'd go to Australia. You'd think that after being rejected time and time again, I'd start to grow a little more jaded, but I love Boise so much that I was confident I just needed to find someone else out there who felt the same and happened to live in a cool place and would want to trade homes for a few months.

As I sent out more inquiries and waited patiently for the offers to begin flooding in, as they surely would, Mike and I planned a less ambitious trip. We would spend three nights in McCall, Idaho, which is about two hours away from our home in Boise. But here's what made the trip really special: we went without our children.

It all started the year before when Mike asked me to edit a blog post. It was near the end of the year, and the post had a lot of positive affirmation crap combined with making the coming year what you really wanted it to be. Most of the time, I think this sort of crap is just crap. The self-help section of bookstores scares me. Anyone who tells me they can help me reach my goals is suspect. Because in my experience, reaching your goals is not about reading how to do it. It's about doing it. Don't get me wrong, I've read a few books that were inspirational and got my mind thinking in the right direction, but most of the time people know, deep down, what it is they need to do. Reading a book about how to achieve their goals does little more than postpone any action on their part, putting a few bucks in someone else's wallet in the process.

Every now and then, I read something that I really buy into. Sure, it's still crap on some level, but it's crap that I really dive into until I'm just covered completely in it. I wallow in the crap like a pig in mud and find myself really wanting to *be* the crap. And that's what happened in this case. Something about my husband's article struck a chord within me. His blog post advised people to sit down and list the things that they really wanted to make happen in the coming year. It wasn't about New Year's resolutions, because anybody can set a goal at which they are sure to fail, and I'm completely over that type of activity. This was more about saying, *What do I want to do in the coming year so that when it's over, I can look back and say, yes, that was really a kick-ass year.*

So I listed some activities and goals, certain things I wanted to accomplish professionally, like trying to write a book without excessive use of the f-word. But fuck that. And there were activities: one camping trip, one huge barbeque, and floating the river with my children. Okay, so we never made it camping, but two out of three isn't bad. One of the most important activities on my list of things to do was to have three nights away from home, with my husband and without kids. The kids would survive in the care of their grandparents.

Our trip was a great success, largely because Mike insisted that instead of just occupying our time by eating and drinking, which is my first inclination, we try to be a little more adventurous. So, interspersed with the eating and drinking, we planned kayaking, stand-up paddle boarding, and a river-rafting trip.

I was completely comfortable with the kayaking, because it was an activity I'd done before. I was pretty sure I could kayak on a lake and not drown. The trip was improved by filling a cooler with beer and snacks and strapping it to the kayak with bungee cords. We kayaked around the lake and pulled up to a small beach on the grounds of the state park. We thought we'd found a perfectly romantic spot in which to enjoy our Coors Light and beef jerky. That is, until a group of people showed up (by land, not by kayak) to celebrate an eight-year-old's birthday party. The kids and adults were well-behaved, but they came with a Labrador who liked to play fetch and then come over to us to shake off the water and sand. It was a no-dogs-allowed beach, but apparently this didn't apply to their dog, because their dog was really sweet. We smiled, wished the kid a happy birthday, and left.

We were in a two-person kayak, and I sat in front. Women don't typically sit in front because they have to, but because we know that men would not be comfortable with the woman sitting behind him, where he cannot see her. Men want the position associated with more control, and in a kayak, that happens to be the back. It's one of those situations where it just doesn't matter to the woman, but it does to the man, so we go with what makes him feel better. Mike and I rowed, and at one point he said, "You know how some women have kind of a weak look about them?"

"Yes," I said.

"Yeah. You don't have that."

I took this as a greater compliment than if he had called me pretty. And I was glad that I was facing away from him so that he couldn't see me blush.

I was a little more nervous when it came time to venture out on the lake on the stand-up paddleboards. I'm not known for my fantastic balance. I was going to be one of those people who did a horrific, cartwheel-like, flailing fall off the paddleboard and into the lake. Then I'd be cold and wet and, worse, humiliated during my failed attempts to get back on the paddleboard. Mike would laugh throughout the ordeal and probably wish he had a camera with which to record my folly, so that at least he'd have something to post on YouTube. But I never fell off. And we paddled successfully around the lake, stopping every so often to drift and again enjoy a romantic Coors Light from the cooler we'd strapped to his paddleboard.

The entire trip was a success, and the hotel was thankfully not scary. It had a pool and spa, which always sounds like a good idea until you remember that you don't really want to hot tub with strangers and other people's children, after all. McCall was marred only by the rude behavior of the head waitress at the McCall Shore Lodge hotel. The waitress in question was either having a really bad day, enjoys acting superior because that's all she has to cling to in life, or is so burned out at her job that she needs to find a new line of work, one that does not permit her to have regular contact with the general public.

In any case, the most exciting aspect of the trip was river rafting. We showed up early for an all-day trip down the... some river in Idaho. It was to be filled with both class three and four rapids. I had no idea what that meant; I just knew that when I booked the trip, I took care to make sure I wasn't booking the easiest one or the most difficult.

We checked in with the rafting company and met our guide, Jon, who informed us that we were waiting for the party of four that would complete our group for the day. Mike and I hung around, ate a Clif Bar, applied sunscreen, and watched as a group of four large, elderly people arrived. *They must be lost,* I thought. *Or maybe they're here to do one of the really easy trips down the river.* The foursome, two men and two women, checked in, and after a minute, Jon brought them over to us for introductions. Jon had a bit of a worried look on his face as he surveyed the six of us.

One of the older couples moved so slowly and stiffly that I had to assume their routine movement did not extend much beyond going from recliner to kitchen to bathroom to recliner. The other couple moved a bit more sprightly, though not by much.

"Okay, so, Mike and Amanda, you two are going to be in the front of the boat," Jon said. Then he looked at Mr. Slow. "You might want to consider changing those." Mr. Slow was wearing socks and tennis shoes. "We have some water shoes in here you can try on."

Jon outfitted all of us with the proper gear, and Mr. Slow stepped off to the side to smoke a cigarette. Mrs. Slow lumbered to the bathroom, grumbling about getting the show on the road. We introduced ourselves to the other, sprightlier couple and learned that Mr. Slow and Mr. Sprightly were brothers. The two couples got together a few times a year. Mr. Sprightly enjoyed walking marathons and was only four peaks away from having hiked the highest peak in all fifty states. This was encouraging, in light of our impending trip down the river. We piled into a van and drove to where we'd put in. Mr. Slow said nothing but fingered a pack of cigarettes in his lap. I tried to strike up a conversation with Mrs. Slow.

"So where are you from?" I asked.

"Philadelphia," she said.

"Oh, really? We were just there!"

"You were?" She smiled.

"Yes, we spent a month in… New Jersey." Her face dropped. We had spent time in Pennsylvania to visit relatives, and we spent half a day in Philadelphia before our flight left the Philadelphia airport, mostly because Mike felt he couldn't go on living if he did not get his picture taken with the statue of Rocky Balboa. But I could tell that Mrs. Slow was not pleased, thinking that I'd confused Pennsylvania with New Jersey. This was not a welcome association in her mind, and deep down I wanted to tell her that Philly, like all major cities, has plenty of sucky parts, thank you very much. I bit my tongue and then started babbling on about my home state of Maryland to tame her wrath.

The trip was a blast and fairly easy through the first half of the day. We stopped for lunch and burned extra calories by trying to dodge the wasps whose home we'd apparently invaded. From a distance, we must have looked like an odd assortment of uncoordinated people trying to learn disco. The guides placed a plate of diced chicken on the ground, which served as bait and a distraction for most of the wasps. They gorged themselves on it, and this evidence of their carnivorous ways was disturbing. I'd wanted to believe that wasps are more similar to bumble bees and flit from flower to flower, but not so.

During the break, we also had a chance to explore some of the hot springs, but much like a hotel spa, these are never quite what I want them to be. This could be because I'd always rather settle for the lame spring than risk an interaction with strangers in bathing suits who got there first and claimed the less lame spring. Mike and I sit on rocks in an inch of water that scalds my buttocks but has no apparent effect on his parts, and we make small talk and pretend to enjoy ourselves.

The trip grew more difficult in the afternoon as the rapids became more treacherous. At one point, we had to exit, carry the boat while crossing what felt like a thin, little goat trail over a particularly steep cliff, and then get back in the water. When we began this seemingly impossible feat, Jon said, "Okay, ladies, don't worry about carrying the boat. Just take it slow and get yourself along the trail." He looked at the crew that left him with: Mike, Mr. Slow, and Mr. Sprightly. "Except for you, Amanda," he amended. "You have to help us carry the boat."

I'm glad that Mike and I were the youngest and most fit of all the passengers. If there had been another young, strong guy there, he and Mike would surely have sat up front, and

I would have been relegated to the group of "ladies" whose only job was to try not to die. It felt good to be needed, to have my strength employed. In short, it felt like what it must feel like to be a guy. I'm not a girly girl. I don't want a free pass. And damn it, I can hold my own.

I'm not saying that the inclination to have the men do all the heavy lifting is an intentionally sexist act, but usually that's how things play out in these situations. Men butt in and take over, assuring the women that they can handle it without us having to worry our pretty little selves. And women typically then step aside, because if we insist, then a man usually does something to demonstrate how weak we are by comparison and to show that we are not, in fact, needed, or the woman is viewed as a controlling bitch for wanting to take an active role. In any case, I actually was needed, and it felt good to help out.

Mrs. Slow complained incessantly about the dangers of what we were doing, and I wanted to remind her that she had paid for the very opportunity she would not shut up about. In an effort to avoid any future conversations with her, I engaged Mr. Sprightly in conversation about his quest to climb the highest peak in each state. He was a jolly man with a resting face that equaled a perpetually optimistic smile. His wife shared the smile, though she obviously hadn't committed any of her life to pursuing the same physical goals.

I thought of my in-laws, who were the same age as this foursome, who exercise hard but party equally, and who look about ten years younger than many people their age. Sure, some of it is luck and good genes. But much of it is choice. There seems to be a choice in how you want to age, what is important to you and what you are willing to commit to. And

I hoped that when I was their age, I would closer resemble my in-laws than Mr. and Mrs. Slow, not just physically, but also that my fallback action would always be laughter and not complaining.

As we finished out the rafting trip, we went over falls and then turned the boat to paddle against the current and back up into the falls. There were two purposes for this. One was to get a money shot. A photographer was perched high up on the canyon and snapped photos as we purposely steered the boat into the rushing water, soaked ourselves, and tried desperately to keep from being catapulted out. The second was to irrigate our sinuses.

We did this three times while the photographer snapped away with his camera. I wondered if Jon was going to keep making us do this until someone was thrown from the boat, and I knew that it would be either Mr. and Mrs. Slow, simply because they were quickly losing both the will and strength to continue holding on, or me because the raft was positioned to place me under what felt like a waterfall. But Jon relented, probably relieved that the Slows had survived this long, and we finished out the trip. I figured that when we disembarked, we would load the raft back on to the van's trailer, and that would be that. But the place where we ended was tucked so far deep inside of a canyon that the raft had to be carried up a steep, near-vertical slide, extending what looked to be a full hundred feet before we would reach the top. This was at the end of a full-day rafting trip, so we were already pretty exhausted.

"You've got to be kidding," Mike said.

"I really, really, really wish I was," said Jon.

"How far is that?" I asked.

"All I know is that it's sixty-three stairs." In a near-whisper, he repeated, "Sixty-three mother-fucking stairs."

"Shouldn't your boss install a winch or something?" Mike asked.

"We used to have one..." He trailed off then, and we resigned ourselves to the fact that the winch of yore wasn't going to suddenly materialize in working order. We hoisted the raft up, inch by agonizing inch. At the top, we were reunited with the van and the dry possessions we'd stashed there. Mr. Slow smoked cigarettes, and Mrs. Slow was overcome with a fit of coughing, which I was grateful for, because one cannot cough and complain at the same time. Mr. and Mrs. Sprightly recapped what a great day they'd both had, and Mike and I drank beer from a small cooler we'd put in the van that morning, just for that moment.

* * *

CHAPTER TWELVE

Internal Alarm Clock

One of the best things about hanging out with awesome people who are older than you is that they inspire you about the future. For all of their quirks and the anxiety attacks they cause me in the kitchen, my in-laws have a rockin' good time. They are extremely frisky in the bedroom, which is knowledge that I don't want to know, but now I can't un-know it, so at least I'll be happy for them in that they are happy with their relationship.

In Mexico, a long flight of concrete stairs leads up to their studio home. At the bottom of the stairs is a large bell. You pick up the bell and ring it loudly. This is doorbell number one. When I do this, I ring the bell and then call out at the top of my voice, "Hello, this is Amanda! I'm coming upstairs!" Then I proceed to the top of the stairs where I pick up doorbell number two and shake it until my wrist aches. Again, I call as loudly as I can, "Hello, this is Amanda! Anybody home?" After this, I stand still and count slowly to ten before proceeding, making sure I'm not rushing in on an unexpected scene.

On more than one occasion, I have observed the bell rule and then turned the corner to approach their front door, which is a sliding glass door, only to be greeted with the breathy voice of my mother-in-law suddenly hollering back at me, "Just a minute!" A furious rustle and scurry of bodies and sheets and clothes follows.

I think it's great that they get it on, but why have a doorbell, or two doorbells, if you're not going to hear them? I'm not sure if this is because their hearing is fading or if they are just so engrossed in passion and each other that the outside world ceases to exist. That is, until their daughter-in-law is feet away and they realize they are about to be discovered in a compromised position. Or, as my father-in-law would say, com-promised.

Another friend of mine, who writes frequently about middle age but who also enjoys life to the fullest, warned me that things in the bedroom change when you reach middle age.

"It's a whole different ballgame," she said. "Your bodies are different, there's skin to deal with, there's flatulence. And you have to laugh. If you can't laugh, you're screwed, but not in the way you want."

"I feel like I already have to deal with those things," I said.

"Good. Then middle age won't be such a bitch. You know, at some point I'm not going to be able to keep calling it middle age."

"You mean when you're officially in—"

"Don't say it!" she cut me off, my mouth frozen with the "o" of old, which I would have followed with age. "I'm going to cling to middle as long as I possibly can."

We all have to deal with the quirks of the human body, and mine has quirks that like to voice themselves at approximately four o'clock every morning. That is the time when my body decides to rid itself of any excess stored gas. As a result, Mike and I are often woken by what sounds like rapid machine-gun fire in our bedroom, coming directly from my buttocks. Of course, it is so commonplace that it's not even startling at this point. No one jumps out of bed and looks for an assailant. In fact, when I wake in this manner, I remain completely frozen with my eyes closed, because this is the only way to deal with this particular form of humiliation. There is no possible way that my husband could sleep through such racket. But like a good husband, he remains completely still with his eyes closed and somehow manages not to laugh at me. Because he, too, knows that pretending it didn't happen is the only way to deal with it.

The worst is when the machine gun goes off, I drift back to sleep, and then it happens again repeatedly over the course of an hour, until my husband gives up on attempting to sleep next to me and instead goes out to the living room to begin answering emails. On occasion, after the first round of fire, I attempt to position my buttocks so that the gas bullets don't ricochet with quite the same force and resounding pop. This requires finding a way to sleep while simultaneously spreading them, all of which must be accomplished covertly so that no one is admitting to the reality of the situation.

I'm not always a machine gun. Sometimes it's more of a nail gun. And at other times it sounds merely like an unloaded pistol uselessly chucked at an intruder and bouncing off their shoulder. Just kidding, I don't fart like that. For the longest time, I figured I was the only person on the planet with this issue of chronic, pre-dawn bodily explosions. That is, until I saw the *Saturday Night Live* skit for Gas Right Posterior Strips: They Spread Your Butt Cheeks Apart. I owe great peace of mind to *SNL* for letting me know I'm not alone, though I'm still waiting for the bold entrepreneur out there who will make this little product a reality for me.

I confided in a friend of mine named Kevin.

Kevin: "Oh, that's easy. I discovered the secret long ago. Buy a full-length body pillow. Sleeping on your left side—"

Me: "Wait, let me get a pen."

Kevin: "Sleeping on your left side, you wrap your top (right) leg over the top of the pillow, and it provides natural separation. Kind of like the lift-and-separate technique of the Playtex Living Bra."

Me: "I find it odd that you're more familiar with the Playtex Living Bra than I am."

Kevin: "Really? I don't. Anyway, the only problem is that the machine gun sound is fair warning. With the spread 'em position, they come out SBD."

Me: "SBD?"

Kevin: "You know, Silent But Deadly."

Me: "Oh. Right."

I'm proud not to hold the distinction of gassiest member of the family. Every family has one. One would expect it might be Virgil, but in reality, no one can hold a candle to Sandi's husband, Matt. And literally, you don't want to hold a candle near him, for fear that he might ignite entirely. Matt can clear a room like nobody's business, and you certainly don't want to do your business after he's done his business.

I might laugh at my four-in-the-morning rapid machine-gun fire if my husband had audibly farted just once in the sixteen years that we've been together. Just once, that's all I'm asking. I realize that this is the opposite complaint that many women have with their husbands. The fact that Mike has made it over a decade and a half without me ever having heard him pass gas, and keep in mind we have lived (and often worked) together that entire time, makes me wonder if he is, in fact, human. I mean, isn't this a basic function of the human body? It's not like he belches excessively, as if the gas is just finding another way out. If he really loved me, he'd do it.

Not to say that I don't have to put up with quirks from my husband, but most of his are just funny, as opposed to humor born of embarrassment. Mike is notorious in our home for walking around singing, though completely unaware of what he's doing. He'll belt out "Eye of the Tiger," "Are You Ready for Love," or "We Are the World."

Mike: "It's the eye of the tiger and the fear of the fight…"

Me: *"Thrill.* It's the *thrill* of the fight! You have no fear. The eye of the tiger does not fear the fight."

Mike: "Whatever, same thing."

Me: "You call yourself a *Rocky* fan."

On other occasions, instead of butchering the lyrics outright, he'll use the right lyrics with the wrong song. For instance, he spent an entire evening crooning, "Our house is a very, very, very fine house," but he sang these words to the tune of "Our House" by Madness, the chorus of which is "Our house, in the middle of our street." I corrected him, of course, because it is physically impossible for me to hold myself back from correcting him in this type of situation, but no matter how many times I pointed out the error, two minutes later he sang the same thing again.

Fatherhood has altered much of the content of Mike's singing, but I'm still not sure if he is actually aware of what he sings. On any given day, he will sing "Twinkle, Twinkle, Little Star" and the A-B-C song, not once or twice, but perhaps twenty times. He does this absentmindedly, and when I point out to him that he just sang "Twinkle, Twinkle, Little Star" three times in five minutes, he looks at me incredulously and says, "No, I didn't." As if this were the type of thing I would make up.

When I realize that we're both singing the A-B-C song repeatedly without knowing it, or when I realize that I can recite every line of *Tangled* and *How to Train Your Dragon,* and also that I really enjoy doing so, I usually call up someone from our bank of trusted babysitters and schedule a date night, lest I lose my adult identity entirely and begin speaking to everyone as if they are a two-year-old. A friend recommended the current production at the Idaho Shakespeare Festival.

The Idaho Shakespeare Festival is not actually a festival. It is a theater with a handful of plays every season, and usually only a few of those plays are by Shakespeare. So the term Idaho Shakespeare Festival is a bit misleading. This bothers me, and I was about to mention it to the friend who recommended the ongoing production, but that particular friend was one of the founders of the Idaho Shakespeare Festival, and on the off chance that the name was his idea, I decided to let it go.

On the day of the show, I drove through downtown Boise and passed Whole Foods. I had never before set foot in Whole

Foods, because all I knew about it was: 1) I would like Whole Foods, and 2) It is incredibly expensive. Kelly calls it Whole Paycheck. As someone who often pulls in what would be considered by most as a partial paycheck, at best, I felt like I didn't have a right to set foot in the place. Sort of like the illogic that would accompany a food stamp recipient going out to dine at a five-star restaurant. But we were headed to the Shakespeare Festival that night, and one of the great things about the grand outdoor theater is that people bring in their own food and drinks and often lean toward putting together elegant and upscale picnics. If ever there was a time for me to check out Whole Foods, a night when I wanted to put together an elegant and upscale picnic seemed perfect.

When I walked in, I almost turned around and walked out. After picking up a basket, I saw a case with fresh salsa and guacamole. Guacamole seemed like a great start to our picnic, until I lifted up the little container and saw that it was priced at eleven dollars. I'm sure it was fantastic guacamole that would have plunged us into a prolonged state of ecstasy, but come on, it's still just mashed up, overripe avocado. I didn't leave, returned the guacamole to its shelf, nestled in with other things I couldn't afford, and continued to make my way through the store, locating items that wouldn't put me in the poorhouse. When I checked out, I noticed that the couple behind me in line, with bedhead, pajama pants, and facial sores that indicated an affinity for methamphetamine, shopped there too. Not that I have anything in common with people who wander in public with bedhead (I have plenty of hats) or in pajama pants (which I think should be illegal when worn outside of the home) or who have an affinity for meth (my skin is bad enough without the assistance of illegal drugs), but the presence of this couple at least made me feel that I was allowed to be there. Whole Foods was not exclusively for the rich, incredibly buff women buying quinoa and looking stunning in two-hundred-dollar yoga pants from Lululemon that accentuate the fact that their thighs do not touch.

I put together a picnic of salsa (cheaper than the guac), chips, veggies, dips, shrimp, smoked salmon, tiramisu, and of course champagne. Okay, it wasn't real champagne, because who can afford real champagne? And the shrimp may have been reduced for quick sale. As we left the house that evening, Mike took a peek inside the cooler and discreetly added two cans of Coors Light, lest we begin to feel too classy, and in case one bottle of sparkling wine proved insufficient. We arrived at the Shakespeare Festival and enjoyed our picnic. Well we enjoyed the champagne. Aside from dessert, the rest of the Whole Foods fare was mediocre. Maybe I should have gone for the guac. Maybe the items I chose were not expensive enough, because they just weren't very good. And I expected the Whole Foods items to be better than awesome. I expected to instantly be overwhelmed by the desire to return to Whole Foods and develop a taste for sprouted things and all things organic.

When the play began, we realized that the one blanket we had brought with us may not be sufficient. The wind whipped through the theater without mercy. We huddled our chairs as close together as possible and brought the blanket up over our heads, like an oversized hoodie for conjoined twins.

"I kind of want to go hang out in the bathroom," I said.

"Why?" Mike whispered.

"Because it's heated."

"I want to hang out in the bathroom with you."

By intermission, I was prepared to stomp down to the gift shop and spend a few hundred dollars. If I'm cold enough, questions of finances and overpriced items have no bearing on my decision making. I would buy blankets and sweatshirts and hats and gloves. I'd throw my credit card at the attendant and tell him to give me one of everything they had in the store that was made out of fleece. I figured Mike would be on board with this plan, as despite (or because of) his Alaskan upbringing, he is the biggest wimp on the planet when it comes to being cold. But it turns out that his abhorrence for wasting money is even stronger than his detest of the cold. He would rather shiver and whimper than spend money in a gift shop. We suffered through the last half of the show, which was good but marred by the weather.

"I don't understand why all the rich people come here," I muttered to Mike as we speed walked to the car. The tickets to the Idaho Shakespeare Festival were not cheap.

"Well, it's a professional theater and a professional cast. And a real set and lights and all that jazz."

"Yeah, but we're freezing."

"Rich people have better clothes than we do. They're all wearing their North Face."

"I wonder if they make heated earmuffs. Wouldn't that be cool?"

"Heated anything would be cool right now. But we just didn't go at the right time," he added. "Think about if we were there when the weather was perfect. It would be awesome."

"It would," I agreed. "But I bet those are the times when all of the really rich people use their rich-people season passes, and the normal people can't even get seats."

"Could be. Although you know a lot of these people probably aren't that much wealthier than we are. They just fake it better."

"By not adding cans of Coors Light to their gourmet picnics?" I asked.

"And maybe skipping the reduced-price shrimp," he countered.

"I was hoping you wouldn't see that sticker."

* * *

CHAPTER THIRTEEN

Pole Dancing with the In-Laws

In light of the fact that my in-laws are the romantic little bunnies that they are, I thought about recommending the Shakespeare Festival to them. It's a perfect date night when the weather is bearable. But then I reconsidered. My father-in-law is near deaf, so a play would only frustrate him, and my mother-in-law cannot stay awake through the opening credits of a movie. Remaining conscious through a three-hour production would surely be impossible, and I pictured her slumping over with her head coming to rest on the shoulder of a stranger. Although, over the years, she has perfected the art of sleeping while remaining completely upright. Her head falls directly forward with her chin resting on her chest, or tips completely back, leaving her mouth wide open and snoring. Both of these positions are accompanied by her arms folded across her chest in front of her. This happens so often that all family and friends are aware of the fact that if you are having a conversation with her and she crosses her arms, she may be preparing to fall asleep.

Nana and I took the girls to the movie theater to see *Cloudy with a Chance of Meatballs 2,* or as my mother-in-law told my father-in-law, "It was called *Cloudy and Meatballs."* When she mangles words or the titles of things in this manner, it never occurs to her that the words she's saying, the version she's turned it into, don't make any sense. Sure, *Cloudy with a Chance of Meatballs* might sound odd, but it's still recognizable as a variation on a weather forecast, while I can find no way of turning *Cloudy and Meatballs* into anything relatable.

We entered the theater, and I knew we were in trouble. Unlike the cheap theater, where I usually take my children, this was a big fancy theater with comfy chairs that even reclined a little. As I suspected, Nana was out cold within a few minutes. I looked over the heads of my children to see her, arms folded across her chest, head still in the perfect position as if she was watching the movie, and her eyes closed. She somehow manages in this position to remain smiling. She looks as if she's really enjoying the movie, and I wonder if she's practiced keeping the smile in place so that if someone glances at her, maybe they won't notice that her eyes are closed and instead will assume she's having a really great time. I peered over at her half a dozen times throughout the movie. Sometimes her eyes would be open, and sometimes not, so that by the end of the film I wondered what on earth she had made of the storyline. *Cloudy with a Chance of Meatballs 2* has a plot that's complex enough for an animated flick, without sleeping at various intervals throughout.

It's not that she suffers from narcolepsy, just that she spends a ridiculous amount of energy playing with her grandchildren, teaching Zumba, running errands, or generally taking care of the rest of us. If she remains still in one position for too long, her body shuts down. No, the Shakespeare Festival would not be a good fit for the in-laws.

The following week, my mother-in-law took me out to lunch for my birthday. Sandi joined in, and the three of us met at a new Italian place downtown.

"Chello, everyone," Sandi said as she arrived.

"You look tired," Nana commented.

"Well, it was stupid. I stayed up too late watching... oh, what's it called?"

"*Game of Thorns?*" Nana suggested.

As hard as I bit my tongue, I couldn't help but begin to laugh.

"Oh no," said Nana. "Did I say it wrong?"

"Yes," Sandi confirmed.

"I'm getting to the point where I'm afraid to speak around you," she said to me. "Because I know you won't ever forget it. You've got that iron-class memory."

Sandi and I giggled more.

"What now?" Nana asked.

Sandi attempted to correct her. "Mom, it's iron *clasp*."

I tried not to snort.

"What?" Sandi asked. "Did I say it wrong too? Isn't it iron clasp? Like a clasp that's really strong?"

"Iron *clad*," I said.

"Oh, well that's dumb," said Sandi.

We sat at an outdoor table along a busy street, which presented the opportunity for plenty of people watching. I don't enjoy people watching with my in-laws unless we are doing it from a great distance, because both Sandi and her mother stare unabashedly at other people, for so long and without blinking that it becomes uncomfortable. On top of this, Sandi often stares at people and judges them wordlessly with her expression.

Two girls walked down the street toward us, and both had a punkish style about them. I can't remember the details of their dress, except that they were completely at odds with Sandi's sense of style, which leans toward former-cheerleader-now-embracing-Ann-Taylor. She's also a sucker for whatever is the latest beauty treatment. Sandi glared at the girls and pursed her lips, her eyes narrowed in disapproval. This isn't intentional, of course, and Sandi is completely unaware of the fact that she does this, but the result is that she appears blatantly hostile to strangers. This also might be why Sandi got into fights in high school, despite her insistence that she never provoked anyone.

A minute after the punk girls made their way down the sidewalk, probably wondering why the four-foot blonde stared at them with such disgust, another pair of women walked by. One had an enormous pink afro, and the other a huge bouffant. In addition to blatant staring, neither my mother-in-law nor sister-in-law holds back when they see something they really like. And apparently, they really like big hair.

"Wow, what's going on here?" Sandi asked them.

"We're promoting The Big Hair Ball," Bouffant said. "Would you like a flyer?"

"We sure would!" my mother-in-law said, and began clapping to music only she could hear. She's an innate clapper. One just hast to mention the word *party*, and she imagines a party, which of course has music playing, so she begins clapping along to the music in her imagination.

The flyer advertised The Big Hair Ball, which was a fund-raiser for an organization that promotes spaying and neutering pets. There would be a hair-teasing station, one-dollar Jell-O shots, a drag show, and prizes for the biggest hair and the best costume. Best of all, the grand party would take place at The Balcony, Boise's biggest and most well-known gay bar.

"This sounds like a great idea," said Sandi. "We haven't been to The Balcony in ages."

"And I think it would really be great for all of us to go out together," said Nana. "We haven't gone out and gotten really crazy in years. Heck, it's been forever since we pole danced."

I feel the need to clarify that while, yes, I have pole danced with my mother-in-law on one occasion, we were both completely clothed, and we remained completely clothed the whole time. It just so happened that the bar we were at, Dirty Little Roddy's, which I have since sworn to never set foot into again, had a few poles, and in the course of dancing, my mother-in-law and I may have hopped up onto two tables in order to dance with our respective poles. Ahem.

Sitting at lunch with my female in-laws, I found myself shocked that neither of them was shocked by the conversation. Nana spoke of going out, getting drunk, and partying hard as a needed family activity, as you'd expect someone to speak of going to church or gathering for a family dinner.

"Yes, we should definitely all go out," said Sandi. "All of us together. That'll be great." I wondered how Matt would feel about this. As if in answer, she added, "And if Matt and Mike don't like the party, they can leave and go drink tequila at Matador."

Suddenly the family outing didn't require the prolonged presence of *all* the family. I hemmed and hawed a bit during the conversation, not because I didn't want to go out or because I didn't think it would be fun, and actually I really wanted to go to the drag show, but because I thought it would be a tough sell for Mike. Would he really want to go to The Big Hair Ball at the gay club? There are plenty of times when I would rather abstain or do something by myself than try to talk someone into something when they are dragging their feet.

We made tentative plans to attend The Big Hair Ball, bade farewell to Sandi after lunch, and then Nana and I walked around the corner to a nail salon for manis and pedis. I typically don't get my nails done. On the one hand, I wash my hands near compulsively, so nail polish on my fingernails never lasts long. And on the other hand, it just seems like a colossal waste of money. If I'm going to spend time and money in the interest of vanity, I'd be better served by going to the gym than a nail salon.

I'm also perplexed by our compulsion to constantly mess with the human body. Put paint on our nails? Why? The only reason I can see for doing this is to cover up a fungus or something that borders on grotesque and you don't want to gross out other people. Which I happen to have, so it turns out I'm the perfect candidate to get my nails done, after all.

A Vietnamese woman ran the nail salon, accompanied by her aunt, who looked to be about 130 years old. The aunt's purpose was to putter about, take tiny glasses of wine to customers, and occasionally nap in the corner.

"You want wine?" she asked me.

"Why yes," I immediately responded. We'd already had

wine at lunch, but this was my birthday celebration, and I wasn't driving, and I rarely say no when someone offers me free alcohol. After a few minutes, the ancient aunt shuffled over to me with a teeny tiny and precariously balanced glass of wine.

"Thank you," I said, taking it from her and sipping. I'd been silently judging the meager pour until I tasted it, because it was so horrific that drinking the two ounces she'd given me seemed near impossible. "Be glad you didn't get the wine," I whispered to Nana. Maybe I could dump it into the foot bath at my feet and no one would notice. But if I got caught, I'd be mortified. Most people in this situation would simply not drink the wine, but I'm terrified of being seen as rude, especially when I've been offered something for free. And if I didn't drink the shitty wine, I felt like I'd be stealing years off of the ancient aunt's life, just by way of my discourtesy.

The nail artist did her best to handle multiple hands and feet vying for her attention. Whenever she asked us a question, my mother-in-law would answer in Spanish. It's not that she confuses Vietnam with Mexico, nor does she assume that Vietnamese and Spanish are in any way similar languages. It's just that Nana lives most of the year in Mexico, and like most of us who know just a little bit of a second language, she reverts to that language when confronted with anything other than English. But that isn't to say anyone spoke to us in anything other than English. I guess even heavily-accented English is enough to send Nana into another language.

"*Si, si, gracias,*" Nana said when the nail tech showed us to our chairs. "*Primero,*" she said, pointing to me, indicating that I should go first.

Many people would think of this as politically incorrect, but maybe it's only linguistically incorrect. My only semi-second language is Russian. When confronted with a language with which I am unfamiliar, my brain automatically directs me to respond in Russian. Even if I'm trying to communicate in French. It simply can't be helped. We revert to whatever is not English that we know best.

As the nail tech painted my toes, I started regretting the pedicure. It felt cruel to ask someone to be that close to my feet. The aunt dozed in a corner, and I was about to make conversation with my mother-in-law when I turned to see her mirroring the aunt. They both had their arms folded across their chests, their eyes closed, and their chins bent forward and resting on their chests as they slept.

"Mama, I love your beautiful toes!" Ivy screamed when I picked her up from school.

"Can we paint our toes?" Emilia asked.

"Yes," I said, "but only after your bath and when you're all ready for bed."

That evening, I gave Emilia and Ivy a nail-painting party. I cannot come home with freshly painted nails and expect them not to notice, or expect to get out of painting their tiny little fingers and toes. Painting the nails of a four-year-old and six-year-old is no easy task. After painting Ivy's, she immediately poked them and informed me that, "No, Mama, they're not dry yet. Now fix it."

Emilia demanded a complex pattern of colors, choosing five different shades and requesting one on each finger and one on each toe. She sat for hours as still as granite, terrified that she might mess up the polish. She feared going to sleep that night, afraid of the damage she'd do while dreaming. In the morning, she woke with her fingers above the covers, splayed wide, still afraid to touch anything. She walked about the house stiff-legged and with arms held out in front of her.

"Why is our daughter walking like a zombie?" Mike asked.

"Because she's afraid she's going to mess up her nails."

"The ones you painted last night?"

"Yes."

"Let her keep thinking that," he said. "It's kind of cute."

While I handle all of the nail painting that goes on in our house, Mike is in charge of cutting the girls' hair. I wouldn't have thought this task would fall to him, but it worked out that way. After the first time I cut their hair, Mike quickly stepped in to take over the job, being far more particular than me.

Early in our relationship, back in the days of Ramen every night and painful conversations to my grandmother, asking for help to pay the rent (she always was and continues to be extremely generous; it was the asking that was the painful part), when Mike was a student and I was a waitress at Crapplebee's (this was before I realized that I actually prefer scrubbing other people's toilets to serving them food), I used to cut Mike's hair. Money was tight, and it seemed crazy to pay even a small amount of money when we already owned a perfectly good pair of scissors. Mike even had clippers. And a few times it went well, but most of the time it did not. The actual haircuts turned out okay, but my stress level simply could not take Mike's stress level.

"Are you on the right setting?" he'd ask, jerking his head away.

"Mike, you have to calm down, and you have to trust me. And you can't move your head like that when I'm about to cut your hair. Unless you want a big ridiculous design on your head."

"I just want to make sure you're doing it right."

"Just let me do it."

He'd be silent, for a moment, as I'd begin to trim.

"That's not how they cut my hair in the salon," he'd suddenly say.

"And you hated how they cut your hair in the salon, so quit your bitching."

I'd started cutting his hair not just because we couldn't stomach the expense, but it always seemed like we were paying someone for a shitty haircut. The idea to have me start cutting his hair came after one too many disastrous trips to SuperCuts.

"Just stop going there," I'd advised.

Then for a time he'd gone to Tight Cuts, which involved more shitty haircuts, but this time administered by women in tight clothing. Whenever he'd get his hair cut, I found it impossible not to make fun of him. "How was *Tight Cuts?*" I'd ask, dragging the words out in a ridiculous imitation of someone trying to make something stupid sound sexy. "Did you enjoy yourself at *Tight Cuts?* Can you get a happy ending for just five dollars more?"

My evil plan worked, and eventually he got sick of hearing me go on about *Tight Cuts,* so I began cutting his hair at home.

"Just let me do it," he'd say, exasperated with me only a few minutes into the home haircut. He'd stand and look at the mirror and begin pruning his head in spots.

"Mike, you cannot cut your own hair. Seriously, in the history of hair, I don't think you'd find anyone who would say that cutting your own hair is a good idea. That's like removing your own appendix."

He looked at me blankly.

"Okay, maybe it's not exactly like removing your own appendix, but still, it's not a good idea."

An adult cutting a child's hair is far less dramatic, at least while that child is still young enough not to care too much about the end result. And if the child can't sit still for more than three seconds at a time, they don't have a right to a stellar outcome, anyway. Regardless, Mike manages to trim the girls' hair while they sit in the bathtub. He moves silent and stealthily, often while they play and are barely aware of his actions. It's an odd technique that somehow works. If he moves slowly, almost like he's in a parallel universe where time runs in a different meter, they are oblivious to his presence. He snips here and there while they create elaborate dramas with their rubber duckies, stories in which the mother duck invariably gets shot or stabbed or pierced with an arrow, and pretend blood gushes everywhere while the motherless fowl fret over their future, hardly mourning the loss of their parent, I might add. I guess their haircuts come with a fair amount of drama after all.

* * *

CHAPTER FOURTEEN

Do Not Show and Tell

We painted nails, we trimmed hair (well, Mike trimmed hair), we bought new lunchboxes, shoes, and backpacks. As fall approached, so did the need to get ready for a new school year. Ivy was officially in pre-K, which is a lovely little term that bridges the gap between daycare and kindergarten.

I think the term pre-K was made for a few reasons. One is to signify that the purpose is, indeed, to prepare children for entering kindergarten the following year. But doesn't kindergarten exist just to get kids ready to enter first grade? How far back do I need to begin preparing? Will pre-pre-K classes begin forming next? Really, the term pre-K must have originated to make mothers feel more at ease about handing their kids off to someone before they enter kindergarten. If I have an aversion to putting my children in daycare, but I really need some help outside the home, but I was hoping to make it through motherhood without having to use daycare, because that's important to me, this solves my problem. I can place my children in pre-K, which is really daycare, but I can call it pre-K, which makes it sound like it's tied more to education than a service for parents who need a little distance from their kids during the day. Pre-K. Problem solved.

Ivy was headed for pre-K, and Emilia would enter first grade. Both children would attend new facilities. Because of temporary and unexplained insanity, I'd spent Emilia's kindergarten year driving her across town to a school that offered half the day in Chinese. The Chinese program was awesome, but life is too short to spend an hour and a half driving every day when, instead, you can walk your kids to the school that's just two blocks from your home. Emilia would attend first grade at the new school, and Ivy would be in the pre-K attached to the school, which would also serve as after-school care for Emilia until I'd pick them up each day around five o'clock.

I wasn't worried about either of my kids in terms of adjusting to a new scenario. They were used to daycare and other children and usually prefer it over being stuck with me all day, in any case. And yes, that may be because I've had them in the care of others from the earliest possible moment.

My kids' lifelong exposure to daycare and teachers and other children has made them fairly adaptable. But there was one hitch I could not have foreseen: The Automatic Flushing Toilet. The new school and pre-K were, literally, new. Unlike the older buildings my girls were used to spending their days in, these facilities were equipped throughout with toilets that flush automatically. Emilia adjusted to this just fine, while Ivy found the unprompted flushing unnerving at first, and this later evolved into sheer terror. I couldn't really blame her.

I remember being afraid to flush the toilet as a child because the loud noise made me think that robbers were going to come up from the depths of the commode and get me. Yes, they were always robbers. And no, I have no idea how I equated the flushing sound with the emergence of tiny men from the toilet bowl.

I'm not saying my childhood fear was a logical one. So if you take this type of fear into account (maybe fears are genetic, and Ivy has the same one) and then add in a toilet that may flush at any moment, and may flush even while you are still sitting on it, which would mean the robbers would have immediate and direct access to your bare ass, you'd be screwed. You can see how the automatic flushing toilet would intensify these fears. I don't know if I was afraid that they would actually rob me of something or if I thought they'd grab me and pull me down into the pipes and sewers with them. And I'm not even sure if the dreaded robbers were really tiny so that they could fit in the toilet pipes, or if I envisioned them as full-sized robbers but malleable, like ghosts that could thin out and stretch in places, which would make navigating toilet pipes a lot easier.

Ivy didn't mention her fears in the beginning, so I had no idea there was any sort of problem. Then I got a phone call one day from one of the teachers at pre-K.

"Is this Amanda?"

"Yes."

"This is Miss J from Ivy's school."

I held my breath. A call from a teacher at school inspires the worst of fears in a parent. You know, logically, that they are probably calling to tell you that your child threw up or fell on the playground or that there was a problem with your paperwork and could you just fill out one more form when convenient? But the fearful part of you, the part that once feared toilet robbers and grew up into an adult with terrifying adult fears, is afraid that your child is for some reason being rushed to the hospital or, worse, missing.

"Ivy had a little accident, and she wet her pants."

I exhaled. "Okay."

"We were wondering if you could bring in a change of clothes."

I wanted to scream into the phone: "Of *course* I can bring in a change of clothes! And thank you for not losing my child!" I felt like I had won the lottery.

I gathered up a dry change of clothes and set out for the school, figuring that accidents were just one of those things you have to deal with from time to time, even though she'd been potty trained for over a year. No matter how in tune a child (or adult for that matter) is with her own body, they (we) are all prone to the occasional accident. Some of us (me) when sneezing.

So I took in a change of clothes and figured the matter was put to rest. I didn't ask if she was afraid of robbers in the toilet, because if that wasn't the case, asking her about it would just alert her to the fact that there may, indeed, be robbers that live in the toilet pipes and try to get little kids, especially during the flush. Surely I hadn't passed this fear on to her. Surely it was just a random incident. But then she had another accident and another. By the time I figured out that she was scared of the toilet, she was up to three times a day. She'd hold it as long as she could until the toilet literally scared the piss out of her.

"Maybe we should check out that Montessori school down the street," Mike suggested one evening as I dealt with a trash bag full of urine-soaked clothing. "Maybe this isn't the right environment for her."

"No," I said. Moving Ivy to the Montessori school would mean more shuttling kids around, more money, and separating the kids to different facilities. "We are not switching schools; that would be ridiculous. She just has to get over it."

"You're right," he agreed. "It's just so frustrating."

Part of me wanted to hand the urine-soaked bag of clothing to Mike, because unless he took over the laundry duty, I couldn't quite see how the situation was frustrating for him. But I instead reminded myself that my husband is a wonderful man who does the early morning routines with the girls, allowing me to sleep just a little bit longer and pass gas in our bedroom in peace and without embarrassment. He cuts our daughters' hair, plays Tickle Monster with them, does homework with Emilia, and takes on his fair share of bath time. *Stop being a bitch,* I told myself, *and just do the fucking laundry.*

But still, we had to deal with the situation and the behavior and find some sort of solution. I immediately used the most effective parenting tool that I've stumbled on to date: bribery.

"Ivy, if you use the potty like a big girl and don't pee in your pants today, you can have chocolate milk after school." This worked most of the time, because Ivy is infatuated with sugar, and chocolate in particular.

Part of the reason why the potty issue was so frustrating was because the teachers in Ivy's pre-K classroom were not allowed to help her.

"Why can't they just go in the bathroom with her?" Mike asked.

"They're not allowed. This isn't daycare anymore; this is the public school system."

"Well, that's dumb," he asserted.

"What happens next year, Mike?" I asked. "When she's in kindergarten. It's not as if the kindergarten teacher is going to be able to leave the class and walk Ivy to the bathroom and hold her hand every time she has to go. It's better for her to just get over it now."

And really, teachers have enough to deal with as it is.

"We do end up with some crazy stories," a friend who is a kindergarten teacher confided in me. "The other day, I had a kid show up with something for share day."

"Like show and tell?"

"Yes, but we call it share day. This kid speaks very little English and normally never brings anything for share day, so I was really excited that he did this time. And when it's his turn, he pulls out of his backpack a big button with a naked woman on it. It said, 'Show me your tits,' and the woman's nipples were flashing red lights."

"Are you kidding me?"

"Nope, and I had to shove it back into his bag, and he didn't understand why he wasn't allowed to share. He was so proud of it."

The conversation involving pride and nipples instantly reminded me of the rapidly approaching Big Hair Ball. When Nana and Sandi had first mentioned it, I thought for sure it would be pulling teeth to get Mike to go.

"How was your day?" I asked, before broaching the subject.

"Okay." He sighed.

"You look like I feel," I said.

"Horny?" he asked hopefully.

"I was going to say tired."

"Oh."

"So, your family wants to go to this," I said, showing him The Big Hair Ball flyer. "It's a big party at The Balcony with a drag show, and your mom wants the whole family to go out and party together."

"Of course she does."

"But we don't have to go," I insisted.

"If we go, will you dress up?" he asked.

"Of course I'll dress up," I said. "Don't I always dress up when we go out?" It's not like I wear a ball gown or anything of that nature, but if we go out for a night on the town, I'm not going to go in a sweatshirt and ball cap. Chances are I'll get a little gussied up.

"Then yes," he said. "If you dress up, I want to go."

So, we decided we'd go, but as The Big Hair Ball got closer, I started to worry. What exactly did Mike have in mind? It wasn't typical for him to insist upon me dressing up, and I started to wonder if we weren't actually speaking the same language. Was he expecting something more than my usual not-that-fancy going-out attire? Was he hoping for a sequined halter top and mini skirt? Did he want me to look like I was heading to Studio 54 in the late seventies? As my paranoia grew, I decided I'd better clarify the situation, lest anyone face major disappointment. Mike said that no, he didn't have anything in mind beyond how I usually dress when we head for a night on the town.

I wondered why he'd made such a point of insisting I dress up, if that was the case, and concluded that my everyday wardrobe had grown more slovenly over time, to the point that on a regular weekday, I look like an unfeminine, unshowered blob, and he was just hoping to catch a glimpse of the former me. But that's what happens when you work at home for a long period of time. Eventually you stop dressing up. Then you stop even leaving the bedroom, because what's better than lying in bed all day? This is yet another reason why I need a treadmill desk, because I'm way too comfy working in pajamas in bed with snacks close at hand. Mike didn't have unrealistic expectations for The Big Hair Ball, but I think he was willing to go to a drag show if that's what it took to get me to stop looking like a transient.

We lined up the babysitter, I made my hair as big as possible, and the entire clan met up downtown. Nana and Papa, Sandi and Matt, Mike and I, and Virgil and Kelly, who I began to think of as a couple in their own right, made our way to The Balcony. A gay club might seem an odd pick for a family get-together, but it felt strangely comfortable and normal for the Turner clan to take over a sizable portion of the dance floor. Mike and I took a break at one point and stood to the side chatting with Virgil. I fanned myself and hoped that my blooming sweat mustache wasn't visible in the dim light. Matt stood nearby, and I felt a little ridiculous flanked by him and my husband. Both are and were so very normal looking. Clean-cut all-American boys, and there I was in the middle with my hair teased to ridiculous heights and my eyelids caked in sparkly purple eye shadow.

We watched the drag show, feeling curious, intrigued, and slightly buzzed. It ended with a lip sync to Tom Jones's "What's New Pussycat," during which the performer repeatedly ran a long, fuzzy tail back and forth between her legs. An emcee announced the upcoming men's hair competition. Matt disappeared, without a word, ostensibly to search for the restroom. I wondered if he'd see anything interesting there, as on a previous visit to The Balcony, I'd used the women's restroom to find a woman showing her vagina to another woman.

Exposed Woman: "Does it look real?"

Observing Woman: "Are you kidding? It looks great!"

EW: "Are you sure? I'm just so nervous. I'm getting married in two weeks."

OW: "Your vagina is beautiful, trust me. You have nothing to worry about."

The men's hair competition got underway, and men with wigs and excessive gel took the stage next to the emcee to garner as much of a response from the crowd as they could.

"Is that... Matt?" Mike asked.

At the foot of the stage, last in line and patiently waiting for his turn, stood Matt. He wore jeans and a button-down shirt. His hair is close cropped and slowly creeping back to enlarge his forehead millimeter by millimeter every year.

"What is he doing?" I asked.

"I have no idea," Mike said.

The emcee also had no idea and looked at a loss for words as Matt climbed the stage and stood in the spotlight, sporting a head of hair that was as normal as hair could be.

"And... so..." the emcee floundered. "Next we have..."

"Matt," said Matt, leaning over to the microphone. The crowd stood silent, waiting for someone to break the news to Matt that there was nothing big or spectacular about his hair. And then Matt began unbuttoning his shirt.

What I'd forgotten when studying Matt's short hair and receding hairline, is that his head is no indication of the rest of his body. Matt is not only considered the gassiest member of the family, but also the hairiest. With the last button of his shirt freed, he paused for dramatic effect, stared down the crowd, and then flung his arms open wide to reveal a pale chest absurdly forested in a mass of black curly hair. And the crowd roared.

We bought round after round of beer and danced the night away. At least that's what it felt like. In our younger years, before children, we had spent many a weekend night partying until the wee hours of the morning. But as forty looms ever closer, we find ourselves home and in bed by midnight, which was the case the night of The Big Hair Ball.

When we arrived home by cab, I asked the babysitter how everything went.

"It went fine!" She giggled, because she is just someone who giggles by nature, and she could tell that I was unsteady on my feet.

"Can I write you a check?" I asked.

"Of course," she said.

And as I wrote the check, I worried that I would be embarrassed by my handwriting, which would surely be a clear tell of my level of intoxication. Rather than continue worrying about it, I said, "Hopefully this is legible because I'm a little bit drunk right now."

She giggled, took a look, and said, "It's just fine."

The next morning, I woke and, before I moved a muscle, took mental stock of the night before, walking through the evening as I remembered it, hoping there wouldn't suddenly be a reason for embarrassment. Happily, fun had been had by all. When I remembered coming home and paying the baby-sitter, I went to survey the carbon copy of the check I'd written, just to see how much I had embarrassed myself in front of the babysitter. But it looked fine, no worse than most people's handwriting when they are completely sober, and this particular babysitter is one that I'm not worried about being intoxicated in front of. We take cabs, we're home by midnight, and no one is arrested or spends the night vomiting, so all in all, it's a win.

"Did you guys have fun with the babysitter last night?" I asked Emilia and Ivy.

"Yes," they chimed enthusiastically, and the adults in the house held their respective heads, everyone having consumed one too many drinks the night before.

"Mom?" Ivy asked. "Is it a stay-at-home day?"

Stay-at-home days are how we refer to weekends. They are the fun days when the girls sleep in, watch television in the mornings, and we go awesome places like the zoo or the aquarium. The girls wear whatever they want, be it leotard, tutu, or costume with tap shoes, and play for as long they want. Stay-at-home days are the best days.

"Yes, Ivy," I answered. "Today is a stay-at-home day."

"Oh, man!" she said with slumped shoulders. "I wanted to go to school to see my friends."

I was shocked by this, as Ivy has never been the social one and usually wants to spend all day watching *Hercules* and eating.

"But you love stay-at-home days," I protested.

"But I want to go see my friend Sammy," she said.

"Who's Sammy?" Mike asked.

"Sammy's my friend from school," Ivy explained. "And he's *so* handsome." She smiled and blushed and swung her body around in a fit of girlish glee.

"What? When did this happen?" I asked. She ignored me and trotted off, singing about handsome Sammy. I turned to Mike. "What happened to the Ivy who didn't like boys and never wanted to get married?"

"Well," Mike said grimly, "she was bound to develop a crush eventually."

"But she's four years old," I protested.

"Yep," he said, "we're in trouble with that one."

* * *

CHAPTER FIFTEEN

The Ice-Cream Unsocial

Despite all of the stories I'd heard from teacher friends about how awful parents are, I always assumed those parents were the small minority. I figured that when my friend Amy told me about meeting a parent and child at Back to School Night, and she couldn't focus on the child's regaling of her summer experiences, because she was too distracted by the hickeys all over the mom's neck, that was surely the exception and not the norm. But it turns out I just hadn't yet been to Back to School Night at a public school. And I was in for a treat.

School was in session for about a week before Back to School Night. Mike held an open house event at his business, so it was left to me to take the kids. We arrived, and I found that the parents of first graders were supposed to leave their kids in the gym and then attend a mini seminar with the teachers. Then we were to retrieve our children and head to the cafeteria for an ice-cream social. When I walked Emilia and Ivy to the gym, I was a little nervous about leaving them there. Emilia had classmates of course, but I could imagine her running off to play with them, leaving four-year-old Ivy behind in a puddle of tears. The teachers in charge of supervising the chaos assured me that they would be fine, and I warned Emilia that she had to stick with her sister.

I went to the library where the parents of the first graders sat awaiting the presentation. I surveyed the other parents and was shocked to see the level of ghetto. There were a lot of parents who looked trashy and/or looked too young to have children. Then it occurred to me that maybe they were not trashy; maybe I'm just not hip. And they might not be too young, I just might happen to be a lot older. I forget sometimes that not everyone waits until their thirties to become a parent. During the presentation, I saw that a lot of these young, ghetto parents were more engaged than I was, and it occurred to me that I was a monumental asshole for being so judgmental.

The presentation was very cute. It began with a message from the principal that was broadcast to a screen in every classroom. But much of it involved the principal holding very still in front of the camera, repeatedly asking, "Is it on? Is it on now? Now is it on?" When he finished with his message, which largely dealt with how technically advanced the classrooms were, the picture was shut down, but they couldn't figure out how to turn off the sound, so the classrooms all echoed with the piped-in monologue of, "Is it off? Now is it off? Is it off now?" During this time, parents and teachers alike held their breath, worried that someone might say something inappropriate and we'd all have to suffer through the awkwardness of it.

Luckily this didn't happen, and a new video came on. This one was about introducing the new Core Curriculum and how it would be implemented across the nation. But the sad part was that to try to sell everyone on this new program and to communicate its need to parents, the video was basically a big cartoon. How sad, I thought, that our education system feels it needs dumbed-down concepts and cartoons to educate parents on their children's future education. I thought about how Emilia had come home earlier with a flyer from school, designed to encourage families to eat together, and again I thought it was sad if parents really need to be told that eating together as a family will have a positive effect on the children.

As soon as the presentation ended, I moved as quickly as I could to the gym, because I'd been worried about Ivy's welfare during the whole thing. But the gym was empty, because during the presentation, the rain had stopped, and all of the children were moved outside to the playground. I walked outside and spotted them right away. A ball bounced across the blacktop. Emilia ran after it. And behind her, Ivy ran in pursuit, unable to keep up, screaming at Emilia to wait and on the verge of tears.

"Girls!" I called. "It's time to go get ice cream!" This averted the tears, and we made our way to the cafeteria. I thought again about what a judgmental asshole I'd been and how really I had no right to look down on these other parents because of how they dressed or what piercings or tattoos they sported. I'm tattooed myself, so who am I to judge?

We made our way through the line where the girls selected Fudgesicles. The cafeteria lady was extremely nice. "Don't you want one?" she asked me.

"Oh, no thank you," I said.

We sat at a table, and the girls focused on their treats. Within a minute, a group of three other women and three children sat at the adjacent table. The women were the type of parents I would have judged, and I silently chastised myself. They could be fine parents, I told myself. Then one of the women, obviously the ring leader, said loudly, "...and my husband went up to him and said, 'You got a problem with my wife? 'Cause we can take care of it right here.' My husband was about to beat the shit out of him."

The woman speaking had black hair, with the ends dyed blue. She wore a low, tight tank top to fully display her muffin top as well as leave the enormous tattoo "Raymond" across her chest in full view. I looked at my children, who were engrossed in their Fudgesicles and therefore oblivious to the conversation. Did Raymond's baby mama not realize that she was in the cafeteria of an elementary school? Of course she did. She just didn't care.

I glanced over, and she immediately glared at me, as if in challenge. Her cronies smirked, and I looked away. Hostility began to emanate from the table. It was an invisible but undeniable change in the air. And I knew at that moment that if I looked their way again, this woman would try to pick a fight with me. A physical fight in the elementary school cafeteria, in front of our children, because she would find some way to insist that I had looked at her wrong and therefore "disrespected" her. She was one of *those*.

I'm not sure why the hostility was directed at me. Perhaps it was because I wore a wool peacoat and didn't have any of my tattoos on display. Maybe because I was the closest outsider, or maybe they just behave badly in the hopes that someone will say something so that they can provoke a fight. I did my best to ignore them and told my kids to hurry up and finish their ice cream so that we could go home.

Raymond's baby mama then spoke to her son, who was probably in the fourth grade or thereabouts.

"Go ask for another one," she prodded.

"What?"

"Go up there and tell them you want another one. Ask if you can have seconds."

"I don't want to," the boy responded.

"I said *get up there*," she barked. The child looked mortified.

This completed my disdain, as the woman obviously wanted another ice cream herself and would rather have her son go through the embarrassment of asking for seconds, so that she could then take it from him.

The only glimmer of hope I saw in the situation was that the boy was embarrassed by his mother's actions. I hoped he could find a way to hold on to that, to realize that she was horrible, because that is the only way I can see a child in that situation having any chance of avoiding becoming horrible himself.

I wondered how I would have reacted if the woman had confronted me somehow. If she'd stood nose to nose and poked me in the chest and called me a bitch in front of my kids or asked me what the fuck my problem was. Hopefully, I would have had the wherewithal to make it a good teaching moment to my children, though I'm not sure what the best way to accomplish that would have been, aside from not getting sucked in to ghetto drama. Would I have reminded her that we were supposed to be the adults and that she was acting as if she was in sixth grade? Would I have tried to usher my kids out the door while she stalked me into the parking lot? Would I have looked to the cafeteria lady and told her to call the police? Are her kids destined to bully my own some-day on the playground? I thought it was only overzealous fathers on the sidelines of sporting events that behaved like this. I was wrong.

I texted Mike: You owe me big time for this.

Mike made good on repaying the fact that I had to face Back to School Night alone. A week later, there was a morning event called Donuts with Dad. This one was designed to force uninvolved dads to have interaction with both their children and the school. Mike groaned every time I showed him the flyer in the preceding week.

"Do I really have to go to this thing?" he asked.

"No, you don't have to go," I said.

"I don't?"

"Of course not. Just keep in mind if you don't go, Emilia will be crushed and probably cry all day long because the other daddies had donuts with their kids. But no, you don't have to go."

As he got ready to take the girls to school on the morning of Donuts with Dad, I had the sudden image of Raymond or another thug daddy trying to pick a fight with my husband, simply for appearing normal and clean cut while trying to enjoy a glazed donut with his daughters.

"It was great," Mike reported back that evening. "I didn't think the other parents were ghetto at all. We had donuts, and then a guy read a story to everyone, and then the kids picked books out from a big bin, and we read a story together. It was fine."

I wondered if I'd *imagined* the hostility from Back to School Night. But no, it was as real as the awkwardness of seventh grade. And next time, Mike's coming with me.

* * *

CHAPTER SIXTEEN

Johnny and the Beanstalk

When we walked to school in the mornings, we noticed kindergartners walking to school alone and kids who went in sandals or coatless on cold days. This angered Mike.

"In their defense," I said, "maybe the parents have to go to work early. Maybe they can't walk their kids to school or aren't around when the kids leave the house, so they're not there to tell them they have to wear coats and socks on cold days."

"I don't care," Mike grumbled. "That's no excuse."

"It's not?"

I wondered how a parent might enforce the wearing of a coat and proper shoes if the parent had to leave the home in the morning first. Perhaps duct tape could be employed to secure a coat to a child who doesn't want to wear it. But I have a hunch that duct taping a child would be seen as worse parenting than allowing them to freeze on the way to school.

This is one of those instances when maybe it's not fair to judge other parents, because we don't personally know what those parents are dealing with. And the judgment doesn't necessarily originate from a feeling of superiority, but from a concern for the children. And a concern for our own children, who will undoubtedly be affected by the children around them.

Sometimes Nana and I walked the girls to school together. The girls and I had picked out our favorite tree early on.

"Look, Nana," said Emilia, "this one is our favorite tree."

"It looks like an elephant," Ivy added.

"Oh my gosh, I love this tree so much, because it's just so wonderful!" Emilia squealed.

I'll be really sad the day my kids stop saying things like this and speaking with this type of enthusiasm about objects in the world that the rest of us often take for granted. Then again, Nana is sixty-seven years old and still displays this sort of enthusiasm, so maybe it's not something that has to be lost, after all.

The favorite tree was enormous and had what looked like giant green beans growing from the branches. One branch made a huge loop down before swooping up again, resembling the trunk of an elephant. It was a mammoth tree and looked like it would be fun to climb.

"Wow," said Nana. "That is quite a tree. It's like something right out of *Johnny and the Beanstalk*."

"Or, perhaps Jack," I suggested.

"Oh, right." Her face dropped for a moment before her enthusiasm returned. "Look, girls, pumpkins!"

Sometimes Nana expresses an enthusiasm for things that I don't understand. I mean, I get and appreciate enthusiasm for things in nature, like trees or pumpkins. But one day, Nana and I were in a grocery/department store, and after we'd gone through the checkout line, we passed by a display of socks. They were plain white, sporty socks, the type I'd use to run in or engage in some type of exercise, and they came in packs of ten.

"Wow!" said Nana. "Would you look at that? These socks are all white! That's not something you see every day." I could tell that she was gauging how much time we had, because she really wanted to go back through the line so that she could buy some of these rare, all-white socks. It was like she'd found a unicorn or the Holy Grail as far as socks were concerned. And she was reluctant to let them out of her sight now that she'd found them.

"What are you talking about?" I asked. "You've never seen white socks before?"

This is extra ridiculous because both Nana and Papa are retired gym teachers. They are extremely active and often find themselves shopping for active wear. Not like clothes for seniors who walk for twenty minutes a day, but active wear for people who hike mountains and ride their bikes off cliffs and run marathons. Surely she'd seen thousands of plain white socks for sale in her lifetime.

"Well, usually you can't get them all white in a big pack like this. Usually they try to make you buy some with different things on them. I might have to come back for those."

Was she drunk? Was she experiencing some sort of brain seizure that didn't produce any outward physical signs but resulted in sock incoherence? And was it just me, or was she hinting at a ploy for world domination by sock makers. The way she said "usually they try to make you" sounded like she was talking about Big Brother. Should I drive her to the emergency room? But that's just Nana, and Nana's enthusiasm sometimes makes no sense to the rest of the world.

As we passed the *Johnny and the Beanstalk* tree and continued on to accompany the girls to school, we walked by a neighborhood girl who I've come to think of as Cat Girl. Because every now and then, Cat Girl stands along the side of the street and hollers back at her house, having a conversation with her cat for a full five minutes, oblivious or unconcerned that she is late to school every single day. Cat Girl also always carries with her an enormous binder attached to a strap that is slung over her shoulder. This is in addition to an enormous backpack. Sometimes we pass Cat Girl after dropping off Emilia and Ivy. Depending on the time, I either inquire about the welfare of her cat or tell her to get to school.

"My cat needs to go back home," she explained to me one day. "I keep telling her that she can't come to school with me, but she wants to really bad. No!" she hollered then at an orange tabby that sat idly on the sidewalk, paying her no attention whatsoever and with apparently no will to follow her to school. "You're a cat! You have to go back home!"

Another day, Cat Girl walked with us and struck up a conversation with Emilia. The two were the same height, and I wondered if she was in first grade as well. That made me wonder if Emilia was slacking on her work somehow. Because if these two were studying the same curriculum, why did Cat Girl have an enormous binder and a huge backpack, while Emilia managed to get by with very little? And then Emilia asked her how old she was.

"I'm eleven," Cat Girl said, and I thought, *Wow, she's delusional about animals* and *a compulsive liar.*

"No really," said Emilia. "I'm six. How old are you?"

"I'm eleven, and I'm in the sixth grade," Cat Girl said.

Nana and I shared a mutual look of disbelief and walked a few paces behind. I didn't interject myself into the conversation. I think it's important for kids to experience conversations and behaviors of other kids on their own. They have to learn to deal with liars and manipulators, bullies and outcasts, and people more popular than they are. Learning about all types of people is part of growing up and part of the school experience, right? So I didn't say anything but silently thought to myself that there was no way this girl was telling the truth.

Nana and I took Ivy into her pre-K classroom and delivered Emilia to the playground, where the kids would line up outside of their classroom doors when the bell rang. I always send my kids off with a hug and a kiss, and I tell them that I love them and that I think they are going to have a great day. I always want to add, "Try not to get lice today." I feel like now that I have a first grader, the countdown is on. It is inevitable that we will have to deal with lice. And from what I've heard and read about modern lice, they are much heartier than the lice I had to deal with as a kid. Okay, the lice my mother had to deal with. But from what I remember, she had to buy some special shampoo, use a special comb, and even though the problem was all very icky, certainly more to her than to me, it was dealt with.

These days, I guess there's more to it. Lice have apparently adapted over the years and morphed into a formidable enemy. The gross factor of having tiny bugs breed in your hair is not enough; now, on top of that, they are tiny breeding bugs that are stronger and more pervasive than the typical tools we have to deal with them. Now you need to spend weeks using special shampoos and combs and pick through your child's head like an attentive baboon. And now you are likely to have them yourself if your child does. That is, if you are a mother. I've heard that lice often like women's scalps more than men's, so the little bugs plague mothers, but often fathers get a free pass. This seems terribly unfair. And what is so different about men's scalps that they would be unappealing?

I've heard that in larger cities, there are specialized salons that have a more high-powered arsenal at hand with which to deal with lice. Or there are people you can hire who will come to your home for an exorbitant amount of money, which I would be happy to pay, no matter what it is, if that means helping me rid my daughters and myself of lice.

I'm not troubled by the stigma of lice, and I don't associate lice with poor people. What bothers me is that it is a bug, an extremely unattractive bug, living on my head uninvited. The unattractive thing may not seem like a big deal, but it is to me. Lice look downright disgusting. They look like a cross between a cockroach and an alien, which is what I believe them to be. If say, there was a family of woolly caterpillars living in my hair, I don't think I'd be quite as distressed. In fact, I might even let them stay, or try to remove them carefully without harming them. But the grotesqueness of a louse feeding off of a scalp makes the situation that much more dire.

I'm sure this is something I'll have to deal with. I should just get over it, but every time I drop my kids off at school, I wonder if this will be the day they get lice from someone in their class or on the playground. And I look around at other kids suspiciously. I want to wrap my kids' heads in Saran

Wrap to keep the lice out. And then I realize my head itches.

As Nana and I headed home, we passed along the side of the school where the sixth-grade classrooms were, and there, standing among children twice her height, was Cat Girl.

"Well, I'll be damned," I said, and silently judged myself for judging her.

Nana and I had almost reached the house when we saw Papa pulling out of the driveway in their large truck. She waved to him furiously, but he drove by, completely oblivious that he'd driven right past us.

"I guess he didn't see us," she said, mystified that anyone could have missed us.

"Maybe you didn't shake your tail feathers enough," I suggested.

"I already shook it for him this morning," she said. Then she turned to me with a horrified look on her face, punched me lightly in the arm, and added, "You did not need to know that."

"No, I didn't," I agreed.

I know about a dozen people who think that punching someone in the arm is an appropriate interaction. And maybe it would be an appropriate interaction if I did the same, but I don't. I'm not a puncher; it's not a greeting I favor. And when people punch me in the arm, I just want to say, "Ouch, why the fuck did you do that?" But I'm supposed to laugh as if it's fun or endearing to be punched in the arm. At least with Raymond's baby mama, she's making her violent intentions clear, and there is little doubt that she wants to cause me physical harm. I'd almost rather that than the passive-aggressive approach of "Hey there, buddy," accompanied by a punch on the arm.

I have other friends and relatives who hug, completely

oblivious to the fact that they do it in a manner that causes physical harm. A hug is supposed to be a gentle, loving, friendly, completely harmless gesture, yet there are those out there who manage to turn it into something truly fearful. Usually these are really wiry people; they don't have enough fat on their bodies, and their sharp angles are not fluffy and comfy. Also, they seem to have a complete disconnect when it comes to imagining how someone else would feel if trapped in a vice grip. It does not feel good.

The painful huggers can come in all forms. My grandmother at the age of ninety-two was a painful hugger. It was as if she wanted to prove to the world that she still had enough life in her to use her physical strength to harm other people. And that's exactly what she did. Hugged with bruises. When I meet people like this, I tense my whole body and grit my teeth and clench my eyes shut tight until it's over. And I think the tension makes it worse. Perhaps if I was able to relax, then my body could adapt a little more, move with the flow, but I can't because I'm so emotionally uncomfortable that it can't help but manifest itself into physical discomfort, too.

When I drop my kids off at school and hug them goodbye, I feel like I'm leaving them in good hands. I love the teachers and staff there. Sure, they'll encounter a certain percentage of crazy, but I'm accepting that I can't shield them from it forever.

Let me clarify my use of the word crazy. I'm not talking about the mentally ill. When I think of crazy, I usually think of people who are bigots and those who lack the basic decency that the rest of us find so important in terms of living. If you honestly hate gay people or fat people or people from a specific country, then you're crazy. And if you're lacking in basic decency, I can maybe give you a little wiggle room if you are a teenager, because teenagers do go a little bit crazy, and sometimes that's just how you have to deal with hormones. The same goes for pregnant women. But other than that, if you are a functioning adult, and you lack basic decency, then I don't understand you, and you're crazy.

I wonder if I won't be able to use the word crazy in ten years. Is it an affront to mental illness? Will it be what the r-word is now? Will we call it the c-word? And if so, where does that leave the original c-word? Will we number them to differentiate?

I don't use the word retarded to mean stupid, but there certainly was a time when I did. I grew up with the r-word at the height of its popularity. It was how we described everything from difficult tests in high school to boys who didn't like us. And I remember first hearing that it was not nice to use the word in that manner, and I thought the person telling me that it wasn't politically correct was being, well, the r-word. But over time, since I've become an adult and have had children, and have friends who have children, and some have healthy children and some have impaired children, I see how horrific our use of the r-word really is.

At a recent conference, I spoke to a woman who wants to end the stigma of mental illness. And I should probably add that she herself is a tiny bit crazy. But I wonder, in light of hearing her talk and what she is trying to accomplish, if in a few years I won't curse the me of today who talks about all of the crazy in the world, including my own. And really, if you think about it, the same could be said about the word ghetto being a negative reflection on poor people. I don't think of myself as someone who discriminates against poor people or the mentally ill, and I'll be a little bit sad if I see these words disappear, because both crazy and ghetto have linguistic properties that make them a delight to say. The *z* in crazy, smack in the middle of a crunchy beginning and a smoothed-out ending. And ghetto, with the lovely *gh* beginning, the staccato double *ts* in the middle, and the joy of saying a word that ends with a perfect *o*.

I'm sure if these words disappear, there will be others in their places. Language continually evolves. And just as there are words and phrases I love, there are those I hate. I love *douchebag,* I hate *get 'er done.* Because on some level, *get 'er done* makes me think of rape. Okay, not always something that heinous, but if I don't think of violent sexual assault, then the other thing that comes to mind is lazy language.

All in all, I've learned a lot from both adults and children at our local public school, and there are certain rules I promise to abide by henceforth: I will never leave my house in pajama pants, unless my house is on fire and I am running for my life and I conclude in my assessment of the situation that there isn't time to change. I will never curse while sitting in an elementary school cafeteria. I will never get the name of my baby daddy tattooed in huge letters across my chest. I will never let anyone give me hickeys. If I get hickeys against my will, I will wear a turtleneck until they fade completely. I will never wear a turtleneck. Since this contradicts the earlier rule, I'll just simplify everything and never get hickeys in the first place.

* * *

CHAPTER SEVENTEEN

Was That Too Rectal?

A friend and local librarian asked me to attend an event and introduce the attendees to the work of someone I felt was groundbreaking in my field. The author could be alive or dead, classic or contemporary, and my assignment was to convey to the audience the enthusiasm I felt for the writer in question, as well as read a selection of his or her work.

I tried to think of someone whose work would have a little bit broader appeal than my own. I settled on Mary Roach, who many would consider a science writer, but who I tend to think of first as a humor writer, because you have to be pretty funny to write an entire book on human cadavers and make readers laugh, which she manages stunningly in *Stiff: The Curious Lives of Human Cadavers*. She's also the author of *Bonk: The Curious Coupling of Science and Sex*. Yes, that sealed it. I would definitely go with Mary Roach.

I decided that for the library event, I would read her more recent work, *Gulp: Adventures on the Alimentary Canal*, and then choose an excerpt to read at the event. One of my favorite chapters in the book involved Roach's visit to a penitentiary where she interviewed inmates about the inglorious business of smuggling things in their rectums. But no, I thought, perhaps rectal smuggling is a little too edgy for the general public. So I chose to read Roach's introduction. Though I didn't read the section on "prison wallets," as the rectums of inmates are often called, I began my talk with how I had really *wanted* to read that section. Personally, when I first read the chapter, I'd thought, *Wow, that's interesting.* I felt that I was somehow complete with this knowledge and that my vocabulary was now that much richer.

I asked the audience if anyone knew what a prison wallet was, and they said no, so I tried to give them a few hints. "If you are in prison, and you don't have any pockets, and you don't have a wallet, but you want to keep something safe somewhere, what are you going to use?" The crowd met me with nothing but silence and unamused, blank faces. "Okay," I said, "I'll just tell you. It's your rectum." Perhaps my folly was in saying *your* rectum. Maybe they would have found it just as fascinating as I did if I had said *the* rectum or *the prisoner's* rectum. More than a few butts shifted on their chairs. I think they just didn't want to imagine the contents of their respective wallets and purses inside their own rectums.

If you think about putting the contents of your wallet or purse inside your body, as surely this is something you want to consider, at first it seems like the women are screwed, because we lug around so much more in our purses than men do in their wallets. But on the other hand, women have a lot more interior storage space available to us. Having a vagina in addition to a rectum is like having a whole extra shopping cart. I wonder if male inmates experience vagina envy, because just think of the expanded smuggling capabilities that a vagina affords us. Then I thought about how some women keep small dogs in their purses. And that made me not want to think about the internal storage capabilities of the human body anymore.

I talked about how I'd discovered Roach's work through *Stiff*, how much I enjoyed her smarts and humor, and gave them a brief overview of *Gulp*. I should mention that I was not the headliner of this event. I was the opener and was followed by a literary author who discussed his love of Flannery O'Connor's *A Good Man Is Hard to Find*. This was followed by a poet laureate discussing a poet she admired, and a musician who took us on a brief tour of the music of Sting.

When the event ended, I greeted the other presenters and Greg, the librarian who'd invited me in the first place. He's a fantastic writer and an all-around good guy who somehow makes everyone want to be his friend. We'd read short pieces at other events before, and on one occasion, he had his family and two young daughters with him. I'd approached him before my reading that night and warned him that he might not want his daughters to hear my final piece, unless he wanted to spend the drive home that night explaining prison sex and defining granny porn. He'd been grateful for the heads up.

So when he invited me to the library event, he made a point on more than one occasion leading up to it that edgy was okay, but explicit was not. And it was because of this that I decided not to read the chapter on rectums. But suddenly I wondered if the fact that I'd mentioned it was just as bad. In my avoidance of embarrassing the crowd with talk of rectums,

I managed to highlight the fact that I'd really wanted to talk about rectums. Would Greg no longer want to be my friend? Would I be forever banned from attending the local library?

"Greg, I thought that went great," I said.

"Yeah, me, too," he agreed.

"Thanks so much for including me."

"Of course." He smiled.

"But my talk, was it too... rectal?" I asked.

"No." He blushed in a boyish way. "No, it was fine."

Given that this was the second event I'd done with Greg in which prison sex or other uses of the rectum in prison had come up, I started to get paranoid that he would think I was unnaturally obsessed with what can happen to the rectum in prison. But that's not the case. On the contrary, I'm just obsessed with prison life and culture. And what we know about a particular culture often happens to be the most sensational part about it. It just so happens that prison's impact on the rectum gets more attention than, say, prison's impact on a person's weight or hairline, and so that's what comes to mind.

Of course, the rectum is fascinating outside of facilities of incarceration. Just talk to any emergency room doctor or nurse and ask them if they have any good stories about things people shove up their asses. I guarantee you that they do. But I think even this doesn't prove a rectal fixation; I'm just interested in the ridiculous behavior of people. And when it comes to shoving foreign objects up your butt, I personally find that ridiculous. At least in prison you are putting the rectum to practical use.

When I returned from the event at the library, Emilia asked me what I had been doing.

"Mommy was working," I responded.

"So, you were writing?"

"No," I clarified. "I was talking to people about books that I really like."

"I don't like books," Ivy said. "They're boring."

I tried to restrain myself from an outburst. I bit my tongue to keep from telling her how she'd just broken my heart, and who *was* she, after all? Because surely no child of mine could say such a thing.

"It's okay, Mom," Emilia reassured me, having sensed my distress. "Ivy doesn't like anything but Sammy and chocolate."

"I know Sammy's my best friend," Ivy said in a voice far too contemplative for a four-year-old, "but he needs to understand that I can't play with him all the time. Sometimes I have to play with other friends."

Mike and I looked at each other with raised eyebrows. Apparently there was already trouble in the romantic paradise of pre-K.

The next day, we took the girls to a pumpkin patch, which was also sort of a festival. But the term festival, to me, implies something that is free to attend. This place had a pumpkin patch, corn maze, slides for the kids, tractor rides, pig races, and petting zoo, though most of the animals looked like they would bite, and I told my kids they were not allowed to pet anything at the petting zoo. Altogether, it cost about eight bucks per person. And there is no discount for four- and six-year-olds, because, let's be honest, it's targeted to four- and six-year-olds.

We entered, despite Mike's grumbling about the price. In one area, there was a huge trampoline-like thing. A monstrous inflated rectangle that kids ran around on, jumping and tumbling and putting themselves in danger of cracking their heads together. After hemming and hawing from Mike and me, because we are generally lame and reluctant about this sort of thing, we told the kids they could play on it. They took off their shoes, and the extreme type-A side of me frowned at the fact that after doing so, they had to walk in socks across a patch of dirt before reaching the jumpy area.

Emilia ran back and forth along the trampoline, with Ivy always nipping at her heels, trying to keep up. At first I thought that Emilia was running away from her little sister, and I wanted to chastise her for it. But then I saw that instead of running away from Ivy, she was actually just running *toward* any boy she could catch. When the boys failed to pay her any attention, she began running into them, so that the targeted boy and Emilia would fall together in a heap. No doubt she hoped that she'd meet her prince this way and that a boy would propose marriage as a result of her tackling maneuver.

I'd been afraid initially to let my kids jump on the attraction, because there seemed to be so many boys, and everyone knows that boys are rougher than girls. But the opposite turned out to be true. Emilia was the danger, because she would employ any tactic she could to have physical contact with random boys. Maybe Ivy isn't the one we have to worry about, after all.

* * *

CHAPTER EIGHTEEN

Hair of the Corn Dog

"How come no one wants to come to Idaho?" I whined. I'd been querying other people about home exchanges for months, still with no bites, and I was starting to get antsy that we didn't have anything on the calendar for our next big adventure. "Don't they know how awesome it is here?"

"Obviously not," said Mike. "But I'm sure there are plenty of people out there who would like to come to Idaho. We just haven't found them yet."

"Ooh, look," I cooed to my computer screen. "I found the perfect family. They're just like us with two small kids. They'd be perfect."

"Where do they live?" he asked.

"Tanzania."

"Wait, what?"

"Well, we obviously need to widen the net."

"But, *Tanzania?*"

"Come on, where's your sense of adventure? I'm sending them a message."

"I was actually thinking we needed to *narrow* our focus," Mike said.

"I also sent a message to a nice family in Iceland."

"Iceland or Tanzania. That's not narrowing. In fact, it's quite a variety."

"Which is the spice of life."

"Maybe the two of us should go over these things and discuss them before we start offering up our home anymore. Personally, I'd like to have some say in where we go. In fact, I was thinking maybe we should try to go to Florida."

We have friends in Florida whom we haven't seen in years. It would be wonderful to see them again, and of course it would be cheaper than flying to Africa. Still, this was a startling example of how differently Mike and I were envisioning our next journey.

"What about Bulgaria?" I offered.

"What about Naples?" he countered.

"Italy?"

"No, Florida."

"Well, let's just wait to hear back from Tanzania first, shall we?"

"I don't know about this," he said.

"Oh calm down," I chided. "Pour yourself a drink."

"It's ten a.m."

"Make yourself a bloody Mary."

But I knew he wouldn't. While we have all of the makings for bloody Marys, it simply feels wrong to drink in the morning. Spiking coffee doesn't count as drinking in the morning. I decided that the presence of caffeine makes it allowable, on occasion.

The one great exception to this is on a plane. I have no problem ordering a drink on a plane, for a variety of reasons. One is that someone else is always driving. Another is that whatever time of day it is has no bearing on what time of day it is for any of the passengers. Anyone on a plane could be on their second or third flight, so who's to say that I'm not finishing up an itinerary that began in London, and for me, maybe it really is five o'clock in the afternoon, a perfectly respectable hour to have a drink. Not that this is ever really the case, but it's how I justify an early morning bloody Mary in the one setting I feel it is acceptable, when thirty thousand feet in the air.

"Why do they call it hair of the dog?" Mike asked. "I mean, when you're talking about something you're going to put in your body, dog hair is pretty far down on the list."

"It came from rabies," I said. "People used to believe that if you had rabies, you needed to ingest some of the hair of the dog that bit you."

"That's disgusting."

"And it didn't work, either."

"So they would eat dog hair?"

"No, they would burn the dog hair and eat the ashes."

"Well, what the heck does that have to do with booze in the morning?"

"If you are hung over, you're supposed to have a little of what originally made you sick, and that will make you feel better."

"How do you know this?" he asked.

"Because I'm interested in things like this. I like to read about weird stuff like this."

"Sort of along the lines of you reading about inmates smuggling phones and tobacco in their rectums."

"Yes," I confirmed. "That interests me as well."

"Well, I don't care what people call it or how they justify drinking early in the morning, there will be no hair of the dog for me," he said.

Ivy ran breathless into the kitchen, regained composure for a moment, and then loudly announced, "*I* want a corn dog." She said this as if she'd overheard a conversation during which we were discussing having corn dogs in secret and without her. I'm sure the idea of this sounded completely cruel to her, as Ivy loves corn dogs and considers them the perfect food. They are meaty, fried, and highly portable.

"Don't worry, Ivy. No one is having corn dogs without you."

She returned to playing, and I stepped outside to retrieve the mail. As usual, my in-laws received more mail at our home than we did.

"Oh that's a shame," I said. "It looks like your dad got a letter from his hunting buddy." It was a shame because my in-laws had left the day before. Fall was upon us, and they'd packed up their things, vacated our basement, and begun their yearly migration back down to their home in Mexico. I decided to open the envelope, because it's understood that I handle any urgent matters. If it contained something my father-in-law should know about, I would find out and relay the information. In a way, I've become a secretary of sorts for them. And they pay me in free babysitting.

The envelope contained four sheets of paper. The first was a cover letter, a scribbled message to my father-in-law from his hunting buddy, thanking him for helping make it such a memorable trip. The other three sheets of paper appeared to be notes from the hunting trip that my father-in-law had made for himself. *I should put these aside for him,* I thought. But I decided instead to read them. The notes detailed some of the more difficult issues they'd had to tackle during their hunt.

Day One
Learning how to tie up hammock
Learning how to get in hammock (difficult)
Upside down in hammock after broken tie, can't get out, up or down
Getting up to pee in dark and getting back in hammock (difficult)

It was obvious to me that wrestling with the hammock dominated day one. There was no mention of eating or hiking or hunting; it all revolved around the hammock. This had been of great concern to my father-in-law before the trip. Was the hammock going to be comfortable? Could he really spend nine consecutive nights in a hammock without completely wrenching his back? But in the end, it wasn't the comfort of the hammock that was a problem; it was entering, exiting, and getting trapped in the hammock.

Day Two
Cow shit in all our sources of drinking water
Cow pies underfoot everywhere
Wanted to nap
Brian jumped a bull and two cows
Running around setting up tarps
Thunderstorms, lightning, sleeping bags got wet
Concerned about issue of water supply

Day two seemed awfully early in the trip to have concerns over water supply. I've always thought of water as pretty darn essential to human survival. Cow shit in the water supply was apparently a problem. Were they accidentally hunting on someone's farm land? And if so, why not accidentally shoot a cow, bring home some ground beef and tri-tip and filet, and call it a day?

I have to believe that getting a cow would be a lot easier than tracking an elk, but I guess that whole don't-shoot-another-man's-cow thing should be taken pretty seriously. I was startled by the entry of "Brian jumped a bull and two cows." The word jump in my mind has two meanings. To leap over or to attack. These men were bow hunting, but this made it sound as if Brian was sneaking up on the animals and starting a street fight. Or was cow jumping something like cow tipping? And were they referring to bull elk and cow elk, or did this have more to do with the aforementioned and disruptive cattle? Did he want to beat up a few of the cattle as a warning for them to stop shitting in the streams they had planned on accessing for drinking water?

Day Three
Up at 4:30
Cup of coffee and a boiled egg
Climbed to 7,000 feet
Almost trampled by running deer
Rainwater from tarps solved fresh water issue

I thought it interesting that here my father-in-law finally remarked about the food. He is a man who eats often, and when he's in the house, it's not unusual to hear the microwave beeping repeatedly, so much so that I've wondered if there's a way to dismantle the beep. He doesn't need the beep anyway. He's deaf to high-pitched noises, and when he microwaves something, he usually stands directly in front of the microwave, waiting for whatever is in there to be done. He's not reliant on the beep, but the beep echoes through our home in a continuous and obnoxious noise, letting us know that we'll have to scrape eggs out of our coffee mugs later. Because my father-in-law is addicted to eggs, and specifically, he poaches the eggs by microwaving them in a coffee mug. Usually my favorite mug, which is a souvenir from Alcatraz.

While hunting, he'd had a boiled egg. I wondered if I could get him hooked on eating boiled eggs every day for breakfast when he stayed at our house. Then I wouldn't have to hear the incessant beeping, nor would I have to scrape egg out of my favorite coffee mug. On the other hand, the house would be thoroughly and permanently filled with the stench of boiled eggs, so I'd have to consider which was the lesser assault on the senses. Or I could just stop being a bitch and tell my anal-retentive self to chill the fuck out. I still haven't decided.

The part about almost being trampled by deer was disconcerting. Couldn't he just get a deer instead of an elk? It seems odd that hunters apply for specific hunting tags to get specific animals, as if you know ahead of time whether you are going to run into a deer or an elk. Wouldn't it be better if you just let them all go hunting, get one thing, and then after the fact, they could let you know what they got? It would be so much simpler. I should work for the Department of Fish and Game. But I guess he didn't have a deer tag and therefore could not shoot one.

Either that or he didn't have an arrow nocked and ready.

> *Day Four*
> *Up at 4:30*
> *Hunted for eight hours with no luck*
> *Exhausted, thunderstorms coming, want a nap*
> *Brian came to camp, got elk, needs help*
> *No nap for me*

At this point, the notes stopped, despite the fact that they had another five days on the trip. Once the animal had been shot, napping and note-taking and searching for other animals ceased while they dealt with the beast. I thought the note was interesting, because on the same day that he'd hunted for eight hours with no luck, he'd called us to let us know that they'd shot a monster buck. It must be exciting for a hunter when a hunting partner gets an animal, but also disappointing if you don't get an animal yourself. This is where I would suck as a hunter, because the idea of getting an animal myself is horrific. The only role I'd be any good at is the camp cook. I could hang back at the campsite and prepare meals for the hunters for when they returned. But that wouldn't work, because by the time the hunters got back after eight hours of hunting, I'd probably be rip-roaring drunk, because what else am I going to do if you leave me alone in the middle of the woods for eight hours?

I'd either accidentally catch the food on fire because I passed out in a camp chair while cooking, which would then create a larger forest fire, which would surely char an animal here and there, so maybe I wouldn't be such a shitty hunter after all. But of course that wouldn't happen because I grew up learning the importance of fire safety from Smokey the Bear, just as my children learn now. A more likely scenario would be that while moderately sipping an adult beverage, I'd prepare a meal with such a phenomenal aroma that I'd attract the local wildlife and end up eaten by a bear. Yet another reason why I do not hunt.

With the in-laws gone after staying with us on and off for two months, I cleaned the basement guestroom to prepare it for my mother.

"How long is your mom coming for?" Mike asked.

"A whole week!" I said excitedly.

"That's amazing."

"I know."

While Mike's parents stay for a season, my mother begins to panic and glance nervously at the door after forty-eight hours. This is partly a hankering to get back to her own space and her beloved dog, Sophie, but more a fear of wearing out her welcome.

After I'd remade the bed, I absentmindedly pulled the handle on the sliding glass door that led to the patio, to make sure it was locked. Despite being in the locked position, it slid open.

"Mike," I hollered. "That stupid door won't lock again." The locking mechanism had been temperamental for a few months. "We need a dowel or something."

"I'll take care of it," he assured me.

"Because this is my mom coming. The woman who triple checks that everything is locked every night because she's spent too much of her life studying serial killers."

I called him on it the next day.

"I took care of it," he said. "Not only is there a dowel in place, but it will also serve as a weapon in case your mom needs one."

I couldn't imagine what he meant by that, so I went to see for myself. Wedged in the tracking of the sliding glass door was a pickaxe, with half the metal head jaggedly and ominously missing. It was a gruesome-looking thing, and I tried to picture my mother, my petite and slight mother, wielding it over her head. Then I pictured her falling over backwards from the weight of it.

"That'll do," I said. "Thank you for serial-killer-proofing our home."

"No problem. Hey, I was thinking more about the home exchange thing," he said. "Maybe we should approach people from the Basque country."

"That's a good idea," I agreed.

Boise has a large Basque population and culture. In Boise, the Basque culture is not viewed as it is in the rest of the world. I once took a visiting writer on a tour of Boise and showed him the Basque block.

"The Basque block?" he asked, confused. "You mean like Basque Basque?"

I wasn't sure what other types of Basque there were, so I nodded in affirmation. "Basque culture is pretty big here. We have Basque food and festivals and all sorts of cultural activity."

"So, the Basque culture is celebrated here?" he asked.

"Pretty much."

"You know, in the rest of the world, we consider them terrorists."

This puzzled me for a minute as I considered how much I love the Basque festival every year. Then I recalled a history class in high school in which we'd studied the Basque people, and I remembered that the unit was surrounded by violence and conflict.

"I'm not sure you can really say the rest of the *world*," I challenged.

"You're right, of course," he said.

For me, the conversation was a great reminder of the fact that what is thought to be truth can change dramatically depending on where you are and with whom you choose to surround yourself. And that thought reinforced the idea that I want to travel with my children as much as I can and expose them to as many different cultures as possible. Because if I do that, then maybe they can find their own truth and decide for themselves what they want to focus on in the world.

We waited for the response from Tanzania. I clicked refresh over and over again to see if anyone from Scotland, Wales, New Zealand, or Iceland was interested in coming to Boise. And I wondered where our next trip would take us. Would we find ourselves in Finland or would we be making a return trip to New Jersey? And if we ended up in Naples, be it Florida or Italy, my girls would undoubtedly tell everyone we were headed for Nipples.

An inquiry from Australia came in, and possibilities whirled in my head like a spinning globe. I didn't need a full itinerary to know that wherever we landed, it would be an adventure.

* * *

If you enjoyed this book, please consider posting a review online. It will increase your chances of finding great fortune. That last part isn't true.

I live in Idaho, but I exist in virtual form, too.
    Website: www.AKTurner.com
    Email: amanda@akturner.com
    Facebook: www.facebook.com/AKTurnerAuthor
    Twitter: @TurnerWriter
    Pinterest: www.pinterest.com/turnerwriter
    Goodreads: www.Goodreads.com/AKTurner
    Google: www.google.com/+AKTurner
    Mailing List: http://eepurl.com/J1LYb

I have an enormous amount of warm and fuzzy feelings for the following people, for their support and tolerance of me:

Elizabeth Day, Sarah Tregay, anyone with the last name Turner or Rubio, Kelly Cameron, Laurie Notaro, Jen of People I Want to Punch in the Throat, Elaine Ambrose, Cameron Morfit, Elisabeth McKetta, Kevin Smith, Christy Hovey, Greg Likins, teachers, nurses, and cab drivers. Extra warm and fuzzy feelings go to my wonderful, dynamic daughters. One last heap of mushy love for my phenomenal husband. This marriage thing is so much cooler than I ever thought it could be.

18385345R00125

Made in the USA
San Bernardino, CA
12 January 2015